FATHERDOM

Copyright © 2025 Brian M. Chapman
All rights reserved.

No part of this publication may be reproduced, stored in a retrieval system, or transmitted in any form or by any means—electronic, mechanical, photocopying, recording, or otherwise—without the prior written permission of the publisher, except in the case of brief quotations embodied in critical articles or reviews.

For permissions, inquiries, or further work by the author:
brianmchapman.com

ISBN: 979-8-9929475-0-2

Published by brianmchapman.com
Printed in the United States of America
First Edition

This is a work of creative nonfiction. While philosophical and mythological references are real, interpretations are subjective and presented in an abstract, artistic manner.

Typeface: Georgia, set with mirrored margins for printed format.
Interior layout and formatting by the author.

Fatherdom

By Brian M Chapman

Dedicatio

*To my sons—
may you one day come to know the reciprocity of generational wisdom,
and may you become wiser fathers than I.*

*To my own—
our discernment should not be measured by our estrangement.*

*And lastly,
to the unsuspecting,
upon whom I superimposed paternal standards—likely without your knowing.*

Internal Illustrations & Front Cover
by Benjamin Zeus Barnett

Rear Cover Artwork
by Brian M. Chapman

Editing
by N. L. Carter

Proofreading Support
with sincere thanks to *The Boser Family* for their attentive eyes and encouragement throughout the final review.

Final Formatting Touches
To my loving wife, *Katie Boser* — your attention to detail helped ensure the presentation met the care the content deserved.
You and the boys have been my greatest inspiration.

Contents

α   *Praefatio Nigredo* — A Letter
    Prologue — The Arc
    Mythos — The Pattern

I.   **Chaos and Order** – *Calcificatio*
II. **Paradise Lost** – *Solutio*
III. **The Norns of Fate** – *Separatio*
IV. **Brahman** – *Coniunctio*
V.   **Gnosis** – *Fermentatio*
VI. **Jungian Principles** – *Distillatio*
VII. **Catharsis** – *Coagulatio*

Ω   *Saturnian Eulogy*

Praefatio Nigredo

Dear Phellow Filosopher,

This is a preface, because all serious books require a preface.

In the pages ahead, I will attempt to conjure the Spirit of Order—
if only to dissect it.

The book is a work of order itself.
I made references.
You can check them yourself.
It is a logical statement. A thesis.
Perhaps even an **antithesis** to modernity's established order.

Fatherdom seeks to deconstruct the myths we inherit.
It is serious work—
as would be proper for such a serious undertaking.
For work, we should always take seriously.

Why do I begin this with self-mockery?

Because this is a note from my future self.
Or not the future, exactly—rather, the future-past self,

as this will land in your future—
the one who came after the past-past self,
who, incidentally, wrote the pages you're about to read.

What a strange paradox.
What a bizarre and implausible introduction!

Maybe someday this too will make sense.
And then again—
maybe it won't.

Yours truly,
~~The Petty Author~~
  ~~The *Saturnian* Philosopher~~
    ~~The Hero~~ ~~*Orestes*~~
      ~~The Recursive Jester~~
        some fool

Prologue

This book intends to dissect a complex Paternal and Religious crisis that burdens contemporary culture collectively and present a way forward. As our society erodes its 2000-year-old tradition of Christianity[8a], what common experiences do we share? Christianity's system was once self-maintaining, yet haunting as it threatened followers with an ultimate repercussion if they sought to secede from it.

The concept of "Hell" is reinforcing to the most pious followers. Eternal damnation, and punishment should be afflicted shall an individual find resolve in anything but "the faith." Its dissonance perpetuates it. Furthermore, Christianity is riddled with contrived rationalities that exist in its own vacuum and perpetuate its binary framework. It continues to incite its own degradation for modern humans who just do not buy into the threats of damnation.

———————— ✠ ————————

The idea of publishing a book presented itself early in my life, and though I did not fully predetermine the subject, but rather I came to uncover its message as it found me. I attribute what one can refer to as "a calling" or the guidance of my Muse[9a]. Throughout my life, seemingly menial coincidence perpetuated and imposed my instincts with universal patterns of divination by what the Jungian Psychology school of thought would be considered unconscious guidance. Jungian psychology referred to this anomalous phenomenon as Synchronicity[7a].

The personification, which Jung called "The Shadow" of one's "Ego," is an unconscious phenomenon to be discussed later in the book. Many authors and artists have sought to personify their muses historically. Mine: whose name is meant to honor my unborn twin brother, Aaron William. His influence has been a silent and poetic presence in this work. Aaron is my root to that which is arcane, and we are karmically tethered in this life and the next. Rest well, brother, and thank you for your solace.

The personal details of my journey need not be disclosed in depth. However, they parallel a common burden for many struggling to decipher their position in the hierarchy of the universe. It may also appeal to those who were denied the approval of a paternal figure themselves. For the sake of relevance, I will keep it high-level and abstract.

What is it about this generality that also seems so implicitly personal? Just as Astrology presents solace to all, its message is so quickly adopted by its recipient as being profound and personal. Therefore, it is to be implied that as a relatively short publication, the fallow periods of my transformation will remain excluded from the progression of the book. However, once the narrative of my composition was first illuminated within myself, the actual production of the book was a mere process of a few months. It was completed, yet the final work would go untouched for another year. I could not bring myself to even read it as it contained significant vulnerability. Once I finally felt disciplined to complete it, I was able to read it with "fresh eyes." Recognizing that its message was still just as powerful as I intended it to be in conception, I was ultimately compelled to release it into the world.

In its most simple essence, the premise of this book is my denouncement of Christianity. It is my journey to fill the void that breaking away from it has created. Christian value systems are the foundation of my being, and I was fractured in this undoing.

The asunder I endured in the degradation of the personal relationship I once had with my father also weighed heavily on me. The vein that defined our paternal lineage was fractured. As for his demons, I would come to know them as my own. The role of a father is to protect, but within an existential value system, your father is your prison. Could I be the only one who felt this way?

According to a *PEW research study*[9b] on the popularity of Christianity, 90% of United States citizens identified with the religion as recently as 1976. A significant decline to 73.7% in 2016, and another more recent poll indicated a further decline to 64%. By the time this book was written between the years 2022-2025 the decline seemingly flatlined in the 60's.

To think: a governing body such as the United States has embedded the name of God in its doctrines and dutifully presumed this would be absolute. Yet, in contrast, the premise of God may be hosted as an underwhelming majority just two and a half centuries later. The Great American Experiment naturally would be destined to evolve. Would we dispose of our constitution in such regards if the very fabric of our undone culture be written upon it?

As Alan Watts[6a] would postulate this irony: (paraphrasing) how we could have killed God but believe we can continue to live with the framework of his rules. Furthermore, what impact does this have on our sociological constructs? What universal laws have been superimposed on our natural minds that predicate our reasoning of Christianity, or more importantly, what impact will those laws serve us in its absence?

Or is it natural to assume that the laws of Christian morality predate the origin of Christianity itself? Watts was not the first to present a hypothetical post-Christian landscape. Perhaps this had always been a growing and potentially underpinning narrative that predates the rise of science[9c]. A culture that embraces freedom of expression without retaliation was emerging. Maybe it was always there, but the power of the church suppressed what is more prominent ideologically now.

Nietzsche's infamous "Parable of a Mad Man" Poem[6b] says it best. This is a mere snippet of the original, but I felt it captured its essence.

"The madman jumped into their midst and pierced them with his eyes.
"Whither is God?" he cried; "I will tell you.
We have killed him—you and I.
All of us are his murderers.
But how did we do this?
How could we drink up the sea?
Who gave us the sponge to wipe away the entire horizon?
What were we doing when we unchained this earth from its sun?
Whither is it moving now? Whither are we moving?
Away from all suns?
Are we not plunging continually?
Backward, sideward, forward, in all directions?
Is there still any up or down?
Are we not straying, as through an infinite nothing?
Do we not feel the breath of empty space?
Has it not become colder? Is not night continually closing in on us?
Do we not need to light lanterns in the morning?
Do we hear nothing as yet of the noise of the gravediggers who are burying God?
Do we smell nothing as yet of the divine decomposition?
Gods, too, decompose.

God is dead.
God remains dead.
And we have killed him...."

The reality is God began dying the day that Science was born, or notably at the onset of the Scientific Revolution in 16th-17th century Europe. It is not even that Science is absolute because it continues to challenge even itself. There is no science more relevant than the science of tomorrow, and when it comes, it will obliterate the science we know today, making mysteries of old lore and wonder even more abstract in every revelation.

Our ancestors lived in our Myths as if these served as their creeds, yet they are fleeting ghosts in our modern minds. Science is the ultimate slayer of myths and magic. The dark margins and cracks in our awareness, once filled with wonder, are now illuminated, and we discover they are nothing more than barren voids.

We are at the event horizon of religious transformation, which most of us are old enough to recall but may have cognitively disregarded as folly despite our upbringing. As for the rest of us, we are unaware of just how significant Christianity may have been just a few generations ago. Yet, for all intents and purposes, it shouldn't be any other way because we weren't meant to stay the same. Science surely doesn't change the thrill of pursuing a new, more meaningful path. After all, this is the Age of Science, and science is ever-changing, so why shouldn't our value systems evolve, too?

It is my conviction that I have come to a catharsis that may be grand and complex. I wish to share my experiences with the hope that the world may share this conclusion. May these experiences be relevant to you: the reader. We may use different names, substitutions, and settings, yet all stories seem to repeat themselves—often just in a different context. As a disclaimer, I wish to point out in advance that the themes and chapters in this book may seem to be a collection of radical topics and stories, yet please exercise some patience as the direction is intended, and they are heading towards an overarching summation.

The book was intended to be direct yet provide some context as it moves along. Therefore, the themes that emerge seem to be sporadic yet will constantly reference each other as they progress, all with the additional intention of not being pedantic and repetitive. Fatherdom, by this intention, is layering as it progresses.

It is my experience as the author, having previously read other abstract theories subsequently, find that most present too much substance of conclusion initially. Therefore, it is my conviction that too many abstract theories are presented in the introduction of a book. I share no interest in perpetuating this method as the redundant nature incites little enthusiasm to complete the work in its entirety. It is, therefore, intended that the major resolve of these seemingly unrelated topics merge upon completion of the book. If as intended, the reader, through the lens of their own perspective, may arrive at a similar conclusion through the logical inferences within each chapter.

The term "Fatherdom" is a neonym[9d]. The term "neonym" itself also presents itself with the same structural formation as the title of the book. The prefix "neo" is derived from Greek and portrays itself as young or "new," and the suffix "nym" is also Greek in origin and portrays itself as a "name." Therefore NEW + NAME= "NEONYM." Thus, it is implicit the structure of "Fatherdom" shall be inferred to be a neonym governed by the same etymology[9e].

As to why the name "Fatherdom"? The specifics of the name will be discussed in a coming chapter. In essence, I was haunted by certain dogmas, repressed familial wounds, and a struggle to adopt the responsibility of raising children. Yet, like most, I was too naïve to infer that it was all connected. This is the story of my pursuit of reasoning, a struggle to establish an ideology that works, and becoming the father I did not know how to be. "Fatherdom" encompasses that which is masculine, primal, inherited, and a burden to behold. It is natural order and the divine as we may superimpose them to be.

Mythos

Gods die, yet we mortals often dare to believe they are immortal. Of all the pantheons of dead gods, none are possibly more brutal and violent than the dismemberment of Osiris.

The death and resurrection of Osiris may be more than just a contrived abstraction of ancient minds. The story may fundamentally present us with a deeper understanding of the complexities of our nature. The story, seemingly fictional and random, presents us with an allegory similar to some modern stories. There is something profoundly personal in the vicarious consumption of abstract tales.

The illusory of elements woven together in the Osiris & Horus parable were likely the result of generations of oral tradition until the culmination tale was forged into its final form.

As the tale evolved, elements that resonated with the teller were likely the details they most embellished. If the narrative was significant to the listener, it was again recited with emphasis on the same recurring motifs. Stories in oral tradition, therefore, hold more significance to the underpinnings of their interpreters. It is, therefore, important to consider that the recording of oral traditions was not the end-all-be-all of a story but a snapshot or milestone measuring the narrative's evolution.

I would like to share the tale of this Egyptian narrative now. The reader may decern its underpinnings resolutely.

Like many Gods of Ancient Egypt, the symbolism of Osiris was a changing one. Once reigning as King along the fertile Nile in Lower Egypt. Osiris was rightly the god of fertility and vegetation. It was not until later, by his own undoing he may be associated with more esoteric values such as the underworld, reincarnation, and death.

Osiris' companion was Isis. Together, they ruled the land, but their reign was shadowed by the jealous envy of Osiris' brother Set, or Seth as he often called. Set was struck with violent cupidity and sought to covet the power his brother hailed by whatever means necessary. Without Osiris in the way, the rite of kingship would dutifully be by Set. So, he conspired against his brother.

The usurper Set and a few of his trusted coconspirators had contrived an elaborate ploy to convince Osiris to climb into a lead box. Once inside, Set immediately entombed his brother alive and cast him into the Nile River.

Isis: Osiris' wife searched long and hard for him before finding his body. By her loving grace, he was resurrected. Set: upon discovering his brother was alive once more, he sought to destroy him again. This time, he dismembered him and spread his pieces throughout the land.

Isis, again in desperation for her loving companion, sought to resurrect her husband. She successfully recovered his body parts from across the land, with the sole exception of his penis. Unfortunately, it was consumed by a fish of the Nile.

With the exclusion of his penis, Osiris was alive. Set persisted in his efforts by banishing Osiris to the underworld as his final attempt to destroy him and maintain control. As a consequence of his brother's persistent insurrection, Osiris would be fated to rule the underworld. It was a mutiny and fratricide of the highest order.

Horus, the son of Isis and Osiris, would come of age and seek revenge on Set and reclaim the throne. A battle that lasted decades and consisted of magic, combat, and even a boat race. Finality would result in Set's defeat. But not without Horus losing his eye as Set rips it out.

By determination for all that is good, Set endures defeat. Exiled from the land, he yields as Horus rightfully ascends the throne. The god Thoth restores Horus' left eye, taken in battle. With his sight restored, Horus descends into the underworld to offer the eye to his father, vindicating him.

Chaos and Order – *Calcificatio*

The motif of Chaos and Order is timeless and recurring. In a sense, there is no more elementary basis for good and evil or known and unknown. However, though these universal principles are self-evident, they are not as binary as just "good or evil." Traditional Taoism[6c] ideology denotes that these forces are, in essence, equal and opposing forces that express the duality of all known phenomena.[16]

Dr Jordan Peterson has been a major influence on my work here and I need to properly give him credit for his inspiration. Peterson is a Canadian clinical Psychologist responsible for creating a movement of existential conservatism when he first introduced his book that was tailored for the public as opposed to his prior scholarly works. 12 Rules for Life: An Antidote for

Chaos. Prior to that he wrote his Magnum Opus: Maps of Meaning, which was not tailored to the mainstream reader.

Since 12 Rules for Life, Peterson has appeared on multiple media platforms as a spokesperson for Western thought and even published a sequel, Beyond Order: 12 More Rules for Life. Each book references the themes of Chaos and Order, yet the former seems to be more centralized on Order, and the latter seems to encompass greater elements of Chaos.[9]

Certainly, he did not invent Taoism, but his constant references to it inspired me to grasp its reasoning on a greater scale. Furthermore, I was compelled to explore the Jungian Archetypes, which we will also go through later in the book. These themes I felt were crucial to understanding my perceptions, and thus, I felt required to compose this book, potentially by indulging my Muse or something deeper.

What is Chaos? What is Order?

In short, energy is all around us. The most prominent and universal forces governing us is that of "Chaos and Order." Furthermore, the most basic principles of which can be demonstrated with the well-known yin-yang symbol.

Yang is represented by the white half of the symbol—a force of Order. Order is, quite simply, all that is systematically governed by law and bound by principles of predictability. It is the energy through which mankind tames its environment.

Yet, Order is not exclusive to humanity; it manifests throughout nature, fulfilling its own purpose as a universal tendency. We have seen when birds migrate, ants colonize, and deer birth their fawns in the spring when nutrients are most abundant. Order in Nature is as apparent and timely as the changing of the seasons.

On a universal scale, consider the time it takes for the Earth to orbit the Sun or for the Moon to complete its phases. However, it goes without saying that mankind is no less a part of this natural order, yet he insists on distracting himself with abstract, self-imposed dignities.

Yin is the equal and opposing force, it is the storm that arrives without warning, causing disaster. "Chaos" is that which is unknown: the realm of misunderstanding. That which derives fear is also Chaos, literally disorder in its proper antithesis being that which is not "Order." Yet the world is not simply rosy red but also shrouded with dark storm clouds. This energy is what completes us, for without it, the definition of Order is nonexistent.

So, throw out what we think we knew about kids playing "cops and robbers." We often tend to regard this force as negative. Sometimes, Chaos occasionally presents itself as a much more intriguing and satisfying incarnation. The colorful pop of street art in cold concrete-lined cities, Epicurean[9f] creations on boring commodity store shelves, or even music are representations of Chaos' ability to charm us when we least expect it. Its mystery shall be brought to the surface to remind us that we shall never know our limits.

Additionally, Chaos reminds us that even the darkness may contain monsters—or rather, that our unexplored caverns of the self may reveal we were the monsters all along. However, we see only the surface of the chaos that ails us, for it is swiftly repressed by Order, shielding us from being consumed by the unknown.

Now, let us return our attention to the yin-yang. There is, as dually noted, an eye of opposition encompassed within each hemisphere. This denotes that within the very core of each force lies the innate existence of the opposing force from therein.

Our very system of government operates on this eternal pattern, where opposing forces create balance. It is no coincidence the terms "right-wing" or "left-wing" are used. However, without both wings, the bird is worthless and grounded—or worse, doomed to fly in circles. A ship pulls straight not by linear perfection but by careful balance of weaving a balance of left and right trajectories.

George Orwell, most notably known for the novel *1984*, also wrote the slightly lesser known yet still renowned *Animal Farm*[4a]. The book was released post-World War II. The story is an allegory told about simple barnyard animals that may just as easily be a children's story. The motifs and narratives, however, would serve as a warning about the existential threat of communism[9g] in that era.

The premise: Major, a wise pig, speaks of better days. (He was a fundamentalist and the catalyst for change in the tale.) He instills the notion that the farmer's ruling is unjust and tyrannical. The farmyard animals are repressed but oblivious to a better way of life. Poor Major, whose ideas outlived him, never saw their fruition as he died early in the narrative. However, he became a martyred sage and inspiration in an impending rebellion.

Thus, it is the manner and the way our philosophies changed the course of history. Like Major: Socrates[6e], Nietzsche[6b], and others each gave birth to ideologies that succeeded them in death. Such ideologies can be immortal as if they were living entities and we, the beholder of thoughts, are mere avatars.

Some ideas can be so profound that they result in the untimely death of a beholder willing to die for them. Socrates was put on trial for his philosophies as they were deemed damaging to the Greek society's most vulnerable—its youth. He was offered exile in lieu of death by persecution; however, he felt so strongly in his philosophies that he rejected the plea bargain.

The fate of Socrates was death by hemlock poisoning as he ingested it to spite the bargain his prosecutors presented. He knew if he left as a fool, his creed would die, but if he died, it would carry on. So, the real question is: did the poison kill him, or did the philosophy kill him?

Major, like Socrates, was a martyr in the name of philosophy. Following the death of Major, his body was buried beneath a fruit tree. This is a symbolic metaphor as the tree lived on to spawn the fruits of his philosophy for future generations. Two noble, young, and tenacious pigs—Snowball and Napoleon—follow in his legacy. Their names imply duality, and their fates unfold accordingly as they lead a rebellion. Initially, the uprising is directed at the farmer, as the martyred Major had foretold. However, in time, the insurrection turns against itself.

After exiling the farmers, the animals have what they could have hoped for. They adopted their own system of order to replace the old way. The nature of their chaos led them to seek order. The initial governing system they created very much looks like a socialist society. Naturally, their own efforts to create "a new" were the foundational steps of their eventual undoing.

What the animals soon learn is the cost and burden of being the proprietors of their own regime is harder than anticipated. Before they endured their own exposure, there were many things they previously took for granted. From this point, it is obvious that the once-communist proposition of utopia was a pipe dream.

As expected by their duality, the two pigs, a once seemingly complimentary alliance in opposition to the farmer, are blighted with disharmony when Napoleon plots to overthrow Snowball.

As their undoing unfolds, what began as a triumph over the farmer becomes an incumbent power struggle, one caught in the all-too-familiar forces of chaos and order. This time, the struggle is between Snowball and Napoleon. As Napoleon embraces the very Totalitarian[2a] regime that he once sought to abolish, we ask ourselves, what corrupted him? Is it so that the very seeds of our destruction are embedded within the dreams of our creations?

So, it appears that we become the very thing we run from. Thus is the nature of the ying and yang. It is the perfect symbol in both philosophy and symmetry. It would appear when the sides are not in balance that radical reform is imminent to restore balance. The Taoists had a term called "*Wu Wei*"[6c] which signified "effortless action" and was only achieved when the Dao was in harmony.

These forces are evident in personal and macrocosmic proportions. Black holes and stars, cascades of constellations, each with their own personifications and dogmatic principles. We impose these forces on the universe as they are within us. Or perhaps we impose these principles on ourselves as we are just as much a part of it as it is of us.

Beyond the myths of constellations, humans have cataloged the stars to assist in navigation and manage recorded time. We have superimposed order on the universe since the beginning of recorded history.

△

Verse two of the Emerald Tablets[5a], a Hermetic text; *"That which is above is like to that which is below, and that which is below is like to that which is above."* The Hermetics and scientists have that in common. Carl Sagan[7b] said it simply, *"The cosmos is within us. We are made of star stuff. We are a way for the universe to know itself."* These concepts remind us we are not *in* the universe; we *are* the universe.

Some of us dance closer to the realm of unknowing and Chaos than Order. Those who barely have clean clothes or can hold down a job, yet some of us govern our lives with such ridicule and scrutiny. Said individuals may double or even triple-check the locks on the door. Some of us may be so neurotic that we place routines over logic. Or we allow Order to guard us from truly living and yet others may just seemingly *"never get it together."* Thus, we can infer that, at least on the micro level, a harmonic balance is crucial for living a life where we keep our ships tidy and avoid being the *"downer at a party."* Don't be a *"screw-up,"* but don't be *"a stiff."*

So, if these assertions are true on a micro level, why not the laws that govern the universe? Good and evil are in constant battle. If the "good guy" wins or has too much authority over the "bad guy," the story is boring and mundane. Yet if the "bad guy" is a sore loser or quits his pursuit of trying to come back, the story ends. We do not want the story to end, do we? And thus, we come to recognize the universe itself is in just as much a similar state of balance.

CERN[7c], the European research facility operating the world-renowned Large Hadron Collider, hosts a statue of Nataraja[8b]—presenting a somewhat philosophical yet ironic statement to the world of nuclear physics. The Nataraja is a classic symbol in Hindu mythology, depicting the Hindu god Shiva performing his cosmic dance while balanced upon the head of the ignorant fool. His dance of destruction is, equally, a dance of re-creation.

However, if this is intended as an inside joke to lighten the hearts of physicists tasked with the weighty role of "playing God," the implications may not be received with the same humor by the innocent masses subject to the future of mankind. The Hadron Collider has been assuredly "safe" and has yielded critical results to theories of quarks and other subatomic studies. However, its association with Nataraja has inevitably drawn public scrutiny and speculation.

From the desire to find balance comes the idea of transformation. The study of Alchemy[5b] dates to Egyptian times as civilization progressed and attempted to quantify the chemistry of soil health to produce better crops. The study also led them to sophisticated methods of embalming cadavers[3a] and, more so, a romanticized belief that immortality could be obtained through their pursuit of knowledge in Alchemy.

The philosophy of Alchemy is also attributed to spiritual Alchemy in a broader sense as the process of change within oneself that closely resembles the required physiological processes needed to change material. Change cannot manifest unless the state of being itself is capable of transformation. Thus, for true change within oneself to occur, a form of death—an end to existence as we know it—must take place, allowing one to be "reborn."

American Psycho[1a] was a graphic film depicting the propensity for evil among white-collar corporate elites in the modern era. Though the film was satirical, it presents several interesting narratives that come into focus. Let's dig in, but beware: spoiler alert! You've been warned!

The world of business professional Patrick Bateman reveals a neurotic obsession with the order that governs his life. His routines, his sterile environment, his pristine and immaculate attire, and the dull conversation regarding business cards with his colleagues all define his nature.

In the business card scene, we see Bateman and his colleagues interacting with typical chauvinistic qualities, attempting to one-up each other with claims of reservations at elite restaurants to demonstrate their social status over another. The business card conversation shows us just how petty and ridiculous their laws of social hierarchy can be as they compare cards with virtually no discernible differences. This demonstrates how they compete to outdo one another, yet they ultimately end up mirroring each other.

Despite the tendency of Bateman and his colleagues to "one-up each other" while ironically being the same, we are led to believe that our villain protagonist, Bateman, is different, waltzing into the office with his Walkman buzzing *"Walking on Sunshine"* by Katrina and the Waves[4b]. An ironic nod to his otherwise stoic and collected demeanor on the outside. The catchy tune acts as a soundtrack for the introverted Bateman.

In the scene: the rest of the office follows complete order unbeknownst of his inner Chaos as he walks through the office without the slightest adoption of the beat that outrageously consumes his inner world.

Bateman's evil tendencies are demonstrated more and more as he indulges them throughout the movie. However, the end comes with an odd twist as he gets away with his fantasy (which is a questionable reality), and the monologue goes:

"My pain is constant and sharp, and I do not hope for a better world for anyone. In fact, I want my pain to be inflicted on others. I want no one to escape. But even after admitting this, there is no catharsis; my punishment continues to elude me, and I gain no deeper knowledge of myself."

Granted, one could infer this as a fictional work, potentially representing the moral degradation of corporate America and an exaggerated representation of one that lives it. Murder is wrong, and perhaps a white-collar CEO with a fetish for axe murders is not impossible; it was likely a poetic exaggeration of the less violent crimes they do get away with. However, Bateman admits he was not held accountable for his actions in the end.

Not only did he clearly not exhibit his passion for music and art or his dark fascination with Chaos, it consumed him as a result. The standard of authority for him and his cronies was different than the typical standard. As a result, in the end, there was no catharsis and, therefore, no transformation. Bateman was the rare example of a protagonist who never took the *call to action*[4c]; therefore, his adventure never really occurred.

Bateman's example was one of a failed Alchemical change. No catharsis: no change. Should the story have continued, we would likely see that his dance with Chaos would be an everlasting power struggle between the opposing forces until one consumed him or, more ideally, he found a balance.

What is it about our shadowy impulses that seem to compete with our ability to be the perfect example of being? It's as if we are asked to walk *as Jesus did*[8a] but are constantly perplexed by dark forces beyond our comprehension. Bateman may have been a victim of this dark temptation, but there are plenty of stories where the protagonist does not.

Another film example with a similar title is *American Beauty*[1b]. No relation, of course, to the previous example of *American Psycho* but another compelling adaptation of the Western Psyche. Our antihero protagonist, Lester Burnham, is confronted with a midlife crisis as his wife, Carolyn, steps out of their marriage. He loses rapport with his daughter to a maddening world, and he continues to spiral as his career diminishes.

Lester has hit rock bottom, and despite the forces that seek to destroy him, he is tempted by his sexual desires for the beauty and innocence of his daughter Jane's friend Angela. Lester struggles to find commonality with Jane and instead seeks indulgence for his pain with the attention-seeking Angela. The two seem to be made for each other, as their pain and loneliness seem to complement each other.

For all intents and purposes, their fantasy collides towards the end of the screenplay as Lester is granted the opportunity to covet the young Angela. It is then that she expresses it would be her first intimate relationship. Lester's pursuit is quickly and abruptly ended as he grips the reality that her innocence is not for him to take. Despite all the pain in his world, he no longer wished to be a catalyst of chaos despite the lust that burned for young Angela.

A metaphor for this theme is portrayed in the scene where Jane's boyfriend Ricky observes a bag blowing in the wind. Jane, like most teenagers, had a rebellious urge to pull from her father; she had been driven into the arms of a man who adopted a philosophy that he could observe a natural phenomenon without taking action to disrupt it.

Throughout most of the film we would be led to believe that Lester had no capacity for understanding this. However, his catharsis at the end of the film leads the viewer to the conclusion that he did have the capacity to observe beauty without coveting it. Lester Burnham, unlike Patrick Bateman, was redeemed as he arrived at a catharsis that disrupted his paradigm.

The old Lester died, and a new one was reborn. Unfortunately, his mortality was limited after his conclusion, but the story poetically illustrates that we can transform at any point in our lives if we are willing to receive the message.

Lester is a stereotypical example of a male in a midlife crisis—but what of his relationship to order? He was a seemingly successful businessman that provided for his family and played the rules of life, at least until the point of where our story begins. He was enamored with that which was unknown to him. The forces of Chaos attempt to work their magic on his psyche. Yet Lester, like many other father figures, is identified with the role of "order." Why is that?

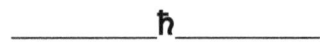

As Dr Peterson would attribute, the forces of energy that comprise Yin and Yang are masculine and feminine by comparison.9 Alchemy would suggest that we are comprised predominantly of one, but until we harness the energy of the other and learn to live in balance, we are not complete. Alchemical symbolism5b represents this theme as the rudimentary form of all matter is represented as *Prima Materia* or the first element.

Further, an Alchemist's path to enlightenment is suggested by the attainment of Rebis, which is portrayed as a human figure with two heads. One male, one female, signifying a fully transformed being comprised of equal and dual forces, balanced and in total harmony. Alone: the feminine forces are carnal and sensual, and the masculine are primal and pragmatic. United, the Rebis is diplomatic and enlightened.

While Yang is more masculine and Yin is more feminine, we come to identify some traits of being paternal, hence the focus of this book. In essence, we all come from somewhere, and if the universe comprises us, we are its children invariably. So, we have certain archetypal attributes associated with these forces. The merciful and justice-bound father and the nurturing and compassionate mother.

We come to recognize these forces even unknowingly; why is the monotheistic God of Abraham always masculine in nature? Why is the natural world we come to know depicted as Mother Nature and perceived to nourish and protect her kin?

We superimpose these values on the world, but what makes them logical is their attributes. These attributes are eternally validated and represented through constant adaptations and representations of the human imagination. This is the intention of archetypes, as they are the complex structures of the human psyche. We will discuss these themes later in the book.

——————— ♛ ———————

Out of Your Mind[6a] is a collection of audiobooks from the late philosopher Alan Watts. Watts was a writer, mystic, and uniquely styled spiritual speaker. The audio files are recorded in a university setting. They are of poor quality to today's high definition standards. Still, if you can survive the rustling distractions and deafening annoyances that result from the antiquated audio equipment, it has a very profound message.

Watts exploits Christianity as being a superimposed perception of man's more familiar system of justice. The church is likened to a courtroom, the Pope is a magistrate, and God himself is a Patriarchal figure of law and order. These are the orders of man, and he likened God in his image. This strikes the listener as a stark contrast from the Genesis narrative, alluding that *man was made in God's image.*

The Sistine Chapel's ceiling portrays Michelangelo's famous *Creation of Adam*[4d], which depicts a naked Adam lying on his back to the left, looking to God, who in turn points back to him. The philosophy to which we can attribute is the idea that it is not "God" that we worship but the idea behind the finger of Adam that points to him.

We have sought to define God, yet we cannot possibly determine he is a white-robed, old man. He is perceived as such as we have determined him to be so. This shows the nature of our interpretations—that chaos is limited to the scope of our superimposed order as we struggle to define it. Thus, it is implicit that God is a construct of human imagination, or at minimum, God as we know him is a construct.

The personification of God as a male authority is not exclusive to Christianity, nor is it a requirement of all religions. Hellenistic religions featured both male and female deities, with some traditions emphasizing a primordial feminine goddess. Even some Gnostic scriptures, which we will get to later, personify God in feminine terms.

The Egyptians had an emphasis on male authority and Order, as demonstrated by the erected obelisks symbolizing the male phallus. Pun very much intended. If the obelisks are masculine in energy, the pyramid is a tribute to the feminine.

These monuments were constructed to immortalize the most revered of Kings and indulge in their pursuit of everlasting life. Not everyone could have a chance for such rebirth in ancient cultures, but those who were qualified certainly would be positioned in these megalithic wombs, awaiting rebirth[3a].

Paradise Lost – *Solutio*

The loss of my faith in God was common and expected among Western millennials. Technology has emerged throughout our lives. The Millennial Generation experienced the rapid technological transformation that followed Generation X, adapting to changes that many preceding generations resisted.

Furthermore, modern Gen Zs were born into a ubiquitous technological world and were always fully immersed in it, so they know no other way. Surely, there are exceptions to the rules, or else I would have preferred to believe there were no rules.

Yet still, we have these generalities, and of them, we hold average consistencies that most older folks as of 2020 may adopt some technologies of today, some more ubiquitous social media platforms. The Gen Zs have the latest wearable tech, and its integration into their daily activities is as seamless as if it were a bionic extension of their nervous systems. The newer generation has little resistance to new systems. Gen Z's meals are delivered by a complex network of automation, app-driven, and no need for human contact[1c]!

Yet the latter may not believe there was ever a different world. I sit here typing this on my iPad[1j] under a smart lamp that my virtual assistant can dim upon request. I know the difference, just as I knew a world where phantom growing pains potentially insight an intrusive thought of impending doom. These dreaded thoughts we fought without a smart watch to ensure me it's not A-fib you're feeling—you just need to stretch.

Society gave birth to a technological world as we adopted it without much reservation. Our parents may have disagreed with an invasive virtual assistant listening to our every word. Yet we have taken the bargain, and we gained so much, but have we realized the value of what we surrendered? People prove time and time again how little they value freedom and liberty over a sense of security and convenience.

Now, I am not doomsday preaching about our way of life or where we are headed. I am more-or-less portraying the disparity between the "old world" and the "new world." Yet, for everything we gained surely there is a price. I think we have gained a ton. I remember a time when I rarely questioned the limits of mortality.

Once upon a time, we played till the streetlights came on. Our parents had no idea where we were or if we were even alive. We were very much alive and having a blast all the while. Now, the obscurity of my children running about in this cold world gives me sudden anxiety. *"These are different times."* Or so the saying goes… but what has changed now, more than how we know each other in abstract only?

Were *Dahmer, Bundy, or the Zodiac Killer*[1d] not before the rise of smartphones? One might argue their sinister impact would have been stifled under modern forensics and surveillance because their games may have been audited before their list of victims was able to develop in full. As I said, we seek security, and my point is these monsters were around then, but we seemingly fear them more now.

Albert Mehrabian[7d], a researcher of body language, coined the 55/38/7 formula. What this means is that the ratio of how we communicate is 55% nonverbal, 38% verbal, and only 7% accounts for spoken words. Effectively, these values add up to 100%, as you may have already determined.

In other words when someone speaks to you, the subtleties of their hand gestures and posture have more impact on your interpretation than we give credit. High-level leaders are coached to give grand speeches and communication while maintaining hands at a line of sight. Why? Because our basic, internal, and primal tendencies tell us that *"man with empty hands is safe"* and *"man with hidden hands has a weapon."*

We certainly do not want the staff or shareholders to think the CEO has a knife or a gun. Does this seem ludicrous? I'm sure you may not have recognized this consciously, but you may take note the next time you see a Fortune 100 CEO make their next big pitch at their quarterly review. Successful people surround themselves with coaching experts who are aware of these psychological subtleties.

These points can tend to surface as we exit a pandemic. We spent almost 2 years developing ourselves and our hobbies. Instead of communicating directly with our colleagues at work, we watched cat videos on TikTok[1e], learned a new hobby, or picked up exercising. Instead of catching *the L*[1f], idling in traffic, or meeting at the commuter lot, we jumped on Zoom or Teams calls[1g].

For better or worse, our paradigm was shattered. However, the smoke clears eventually: between public immunity, vaccination rates, and time on our side, we re-emerge, but under what pretense? We remind ourselves of the value of our interactions at times like these. The power of seeing the bottom half of someone's face. Now, 55% of our daily interactions are right there in front of us again. It's more vivid than ever; we are communicating in 4K after social distancing reduced our prefrontal cortex to dial-up speeds!

So, what of the other 45%? Surely, the words we use or choose to use or a likewise synonym may exhibit some worth. As I thought about naming this book, I pondered the word *"Parendom." I thought it was a word I cleverly made up,* representing "paren" as Latin for "parent" and "Dom" as a suffix for the realm of being. I.e., "free*dom*" or "king*dom*." Learning Latin is rewarding, even for a "dead" language, and has always been a skill I inconstantly sought to develop. It helps to broaden your vocabulary and ability to decipher any of the subsequent Romantic languages. But just as cleverly as I thought of the word "*Parendom*," the French seemingly had beat me to it[9h].

Furthermore, as a father, I felt a personal regard for the role and thus thought *"Patridom"* may be more compelling. It was original, as I still wished to use a neonym. This "word" evoked a similarity to *"patriarchy,"* which I figured may impose a certain connotation that presents a political divide between progressive and conservative ideologies. I wanted to be adamant not to burden this book with modern political discourse.

So, I digress to "Fatherdom" as the term "Father" seemed to evoke some more noble and majestic implication. I.e., The *Allfather*[8c] in Norse mythology, *Thy Father in Heaven*[8a] as in Christian gospel, or even Danny Tanner: the wholesome paternal role model that melted our hearts on the hit TV show Full House[1h]. As you may note, the implications of Order are personified in a Father archetype, as discussed in the previous chapter.

That single-word title: I spent so much time on yet may carry only about 7% of the weight of my total thesis overarching concept in this book. Tone and verbal cadence make up another 38%: well, we had that on Zoom calls. At least we have inflection, and we have the manner in which the individual speaks in a virtual meeting.

It is not what we say; it is how we say it. And so: sarcasm may not be a good device to use if you are deciding to send an email or a text message as it tends to have the opposite effect. So, as we head back to the movie theaters, the brick n' mortars, and the office, we realize the oxytocin that we can generate by simply having a conversation around the water cooler or holding the door for someone.

Why am I making these points about body language? They remind us that sometimes, our true nature and intentions can get lost in the abstract. How many times do we assume the worst of someone else, just to realize after a quick heart-to-heart there was a basic misunderstanding? How many menial political fights do we have to have on Facebook[1i] to admit we would never say those things to another "face to face?" *"Oh, you didn't vote for that guy? I voted for 'so and so'—agree to disagree."*

I have heard very few people calling random strangers in grocery stores *"nazis"* or *"snowflakes."* These are just some of the contrive and irrational terminologies of political tribalism. Again, there are no rules to these things, but the generalities are there. I'm not saying confrontations don't exist, but the evidence is empirical versus the toxic plethora online. People on the internet are assholes, yet those same assholes might hold the door for you one day.

I promised you before I am not doomsday preaching here. The world is not a lost cause. It is simply "different." You and I are not inherently broken, but who is to say we should not seek repair? Hell, if you think we are broken as a society, think of how progressive the adoption of inclusivity has been. The path to equal human rights has not been linear, but it has moved forward.

Again, I like to think there are no rules, and some exceptions surely imply. Across the political aisle, some may insist there are droves of racists in waiting. As if anyone not voting for your guy is *"racist"* or *"unempathetic"* to society's most vulnerable. There is more than just one issue on every ballot, yet we isolate ourselves and righteously defend our points as though we cannot pick and choose.

This is not a political rant but rather a demonstration of the disparity between extremes and our tendency to expect the worst of someone who may not be in our faction.

As if letting those kids stay out until the streetlights came on meant they weren't just at risk of being abducted by traffickers but also of being recruited—either into a communist militia in the name of Saul Alinsky[2b] or, conversely, indoctrinated into right-wing ideology by Breitbart[2c]. We are so far removed from our neighbors that we see them only in the abstract—no longer as fathers, mothers, daughters, or sons, but as radicals of the left or zealots of the right.

Of all the distrust, we seemingly have produced a quandary; we have gained access to a lightning-fast information highway. This is something I would have only dreamed of as a small child. I was inquisitive. Okay, fine, I rephrase, *"I was intrusive."* I was the child who constantly derailed agendas with one haunting word: *"Why?"* Not that being inquisitive is a terrible thing, it is one of my finer attributes, and I shall also hope to further be it so.

It is something almost divine to satisfy the calling of the Muses. Yet, in today's information-dense ecosystem, I will unfortunately forget more than I will learn in a million lifetimes. At least my smart devices are an extension of my nervous system now, and I no longer must remember trivial facts to feel educated. I do not recall more than a few phone numbers, despite never having had to write them down 20+ years ago. I can even compute with the best of them now, thanks to my iPhone[1j] calculator!

Yet, with all this information, are we any more enlightened? Or is our sustenance lost in the substance? We know the difference, but do we care to set a standard? What restraints can we impose on our media diets that we have yet to impose on our caloric diets?

Primitive humans may have fasted for days, hoping to sustain enough energy for their next hunt to be a success or a gathering to be fruitful. Exercise was not a requirement of our early hominid ancestors; body fat was a survival requirement.

Due to advancements in food security, exercise provides a remedy for this new evolutionary quandary. Fat was the body's way of storing nutrients, not an unwanted side effect of overindulgence. Most of the things we ingest are not in nature, so unnaturally, we would have to impose a cardiovascular simulation of what may have been required to attain it in the first place. Our Neanderthal ancestors, unfortunately, were unable to forage cheesecakes and butter; our indulgence in the modern age comes with a price and responsibility if we can effectively manage it.

I will now postulate the thought of what new stimuli we perceive that we may have otherwise not been exposed to in the preceding of this "new world." For the Gen Zs in the room, I assure you the answer is not staring at the wall doing nothing as if there was an imaginary TV in its place. We told stories. We went to church. We told jokes. We might have even walked over to the neighbor's house to annoy them with menial desperation of human interaction to borrow the *TV guide*[1k], a "cup o' sugar," or to return that *Tupperware*[1l].

What do I mean by all this? I mean that the mind is a computer with finite processing power. Limited RAM[9i] (Random Access Memory for the Boomers in the room), so to speak. It's our temporary memory, basically, and we bog it down with so much "stuff." What good does it all do, and more importantly, what did it take the place of?

There was a time when sitting on the toilet may have been an invite to gaze unknowingly into an abyss and ponder one's mortality. Yet with silica-based technology, those uncomfortable feelings can be swept aside with 30-second doses of flashy content, a text message, an email, the stats on the game, or, heaven forbid, an advertisement!

So, we've pushed those bad feelings out and brought in the good stuff. A dopamine-dependent society with instant gratification is the true cost of our consumption. We have removed what is meaningful and replaced it with what is expedient, as Jordan Peterson would proclaim.

What is meaningful? Well, first, we must ask ourselves what WAS meaningful. In short, it was God; before I lose you, I am no preacher. Like I said, I am just your average millennial who fell from faith. If I were Nietzsche[6b], I would say MY God is dead; in fact, I killed MY God. What did I fill my days of longing and hopes for eternal bliss with? Instant gratification. I not only seek promptly to consume resolve for my sudden urges, but I also often consume without knowing that I even need something at all.

I recall my earliest comprehension of The Book of Revelations[8a], and I was compelled to understand it. Like I said, I asked "why" a lot. The Book of Revelations was a huge elephant in the room for an inquisitive child. It was preluding that our impending doom or liberation for our tired lives of servitude and pain was undoubtedly headed towards a certain fantastical cataclysm. Naturally, I was enamored with it; it's like the more visually horrific side of the Bible—like the movies you weren't allowed to watch as a young child, no boring church songs, just the rated R stuff.

My mother told me an Antichrist was coming and drilled me to determine my ability to abstain; I told her I would simply "karate chop him," but then I was brought to terms with the deception he may possess. This Antichrist would challenge my faith in God by offering me the wonders of this world at the cost that would, unfortunately, be my eternal damnation. Not a happy thought for a 6-year-old but a character-building ideology that may challenge oneself for more willpower over their immediate actions in the future; therefore not a bad lesson in practice.

Any righteous self-help book will tell you that sacrifice today means wealth tomorrow. What was this doomsday stuff all about? Was Jesus the OG Tony Robbins[1m], or was the Bible just an early Rich Dad, Poor Dad[4e]?

Still, with this heavy dogma haunting my every waking move, at least on some subconscious level, I did not see enough reason to behold the logic of Christianity for much longer following that not-so-carefree day.

If I had to be honest with myself, it seemed overly embellished to be worth the hype. In fact, Jesus was kind of "cringy," to say the least. In today's day in age, self-identified Messiahs do not have their feet washed by people on the streets or attract large gatherings and have apostles and sycophants. No, they are given anti-psychotics, institutionalized, and laughed about. Certainly, the credibility of any said individual would have been discounted prior to even their first words. If anything, their mother's claims of immaculate conception would have been too laughable to endure.

There are miracles in this world, but they are measured by acts of decency and kindness when least expected, not by magic and mystery. Insemination is not a mystery. It is either penetration or sloppy foreplay; a modern comprehensive assessment of the laws of biology may not have been present 2000 years ago.

Hell, at that time, humankind had yet to experience the plague and wore silly masks to scare off ghosts that may infect them. Yes, plague doctors[3b] wore those horrifying and iconic masks to pack herbs and spices within, so they did not inhale the demons that consumed their patients. This begs to question, were they inadvertently spared from some respiratory viruses as a result? So close to the truth, yet so lost in the abstract and crippled by lack of comprehension. Antiseptics would not even be invented for another 1800 years, and if they had any real consideration for hygiene 2000 years ago, Mary probably wouldn't be giving birth in a barn.

The fairy tale details aside, the younger me often asked if it was all just a story to tell a greater truth. If I don't allow myself to get lost in the details, I may come to see the value of its lessons through imagery and metaphors. However, I was still challenged in practice by examples of hypocrisy amongst those who called themselves the most faithful. These virtue signalers who preached and yet practiced with much dramatic contrast were impressionable to an inquisitive type and not in a positive way.

Even those who practiced the faith devoutly: a perfect replica of the living Christ yet exhausting in their predictable boring antidotes of pedantic expressions. *"God is good," "Jesus is Lord," "WWJD," and "peace" are* cringeworthy slogans of no particular significance and mindless incantations of zealous followers destined to repeat and recite as though their existence depended on it.

Last and worse yet, the infallible offenders of God's word, those who preach and condescend to others or worse. I'm talking about those who prey upon the lost and naïve with heinous acts of sexual abuse and violence against the institution's most fragile and vulnerable members.

These commonalities alone would make any sane person distrust God, and yet, under certain circumstances, some may be driven to hate the institution of God. As an angry teenager, I was proud enough to wear the title *"Atheist."* At the point in which I write this, in retrospect, some years later, I came to determine this outlook was not really a true religion, nor did it serve a purpose beyond disavowing the existence of "God."

After all, it is not like humans blipped into existence 2000 years ago, and the millions of Earth years preceding the rise to Christianity were a mistake that predicated no eternal life. The God Anubis[8d] sitting at the threshold of death:

"I'm sorry, no heaven or everlasting life for you, that's on pause for a couple of millennia."

I often pictured the exponential souls sitting in purgatory predating the New Testament as though their lives did not matter. As if they were waiting for thousands of years for our much more important lives to play out before they could receive their judgment. Waiting, until that final day, but then as if God were to confront the ghosts of 20,000 years ago and determine the eons to follow based upon their acknowledgment of a guy who had a messianic complex 18,000 years later.

The rules were just "dumb" and so I decided there should not be any. But one thing I was slowly coming to terms with was that being an Atheist was about as menial in contrast as it seemingly only served to negate Christianity but offered no answers for much else. As if it existed solely to claim Christianity didn't, therefore giving more weight to Christianity than I felt it merited. An antithesis can only exist if there is a thesis to begin with; after all, why would anyone try to dispute it otherwise?

As Peterson[6d] would assert, *"There are no Atheists. Just those that don't know what god they serve."*

I unplugged a hole. Not just any hole: a vacuum. The Event Horizon is the point of no return for a Black Hole; it is a final frontier for atomic particles; when you remove a paradigm, the mind desperately tries to replace it with a new narrative. There was a black hole, alright, and it was sucking anything that would come close enough to draw it in.

Like The Fall of Satan in John Milton's *Paradise Lost*[6f] I too felt like I had descended from Heaven. Even Satan, at one time, adored God. However, he sought to challenge the hierarchy of things, and he was exiled as a result.

So, it stands to reason: why was God's love so conditional and devoid of confrontation? Was the philosophy of his premise too frail to bear opposition? What are the convictions of God if not justifiable but enforced by dismissal? Satan said it best:

"Here at least we shall be free; the Almighty hath not built.

Here for his envy, will not drive us hence:

Here we may reign secure and in my choice

To reign is worth ambition, though in Hell:

Better to reign in Hell than serve in Heaven."

The Norns of Fate – *Separatio*

At the base of Yggdrasil[8c], the great Tree of Life, the three sisters of fate carry buckets of water to nourish its roots. Thus, the lore of the Norns unfolds—so the tree may not wither, nor its roots decay. Ancient Nordic cultures believed that the universe could be attributed to a great tree. Harbored within The Great Tree of Life were nine realms.

Of these realms was most notably Midgard: The prefix *"Mid"* signifies its position as the middle realm of existence, while *"gard"* derives from the Old Norse "garðr," meaning enclosure or stronghold. Thus, Midgard translates to *"Middle Enclosure"*—a realm protected amidst the vast cosmic structure of Yggdrasil. This was the domain of humanity. It was the realm that ancient Vikings would occupy throughout their time on Earth.

Because the Vikings upheld such strong regard for the appointments that The Sisters of Fate held for us, there was not much reason to believe that our fates weren't pre-determined. The will of an individual resides in their conflict to journey towards recognizing that fate and fulfilling their destiny. Sometimes, denial can be futile. The Norns were often portrayed as cloaked shadowy figures who were not only responsible for keeping the roots of the great Yggdrasil damp, but they were also the seamstresses who wove the fabric of time itself. It was quite a tall task for three old ladies.

But the Norns were not the only mythological characters upheld with high regard. Although they were thought to be resolute and exempt from the quandaries that faced mankind, they acted in counsel and solace to the gods of ancient Norway or as often referred to as "Vikings." There was a pantheon of gods that comprised the mythology of the Vikings. What I find most compelling is the fact that they were not exempt from the same curses that plague humanity. The Norse equivalent of Christianity's Book of Revelations was the story of Ragnarök. In Ragnarök: the Allfather, *Odin* himself is consumed by a giant wolf named Fenrir. Odin and the other gods reigned in Asgard, which is akin to the Christian concept of "Heaven."

For the Gods, it was merely as if their conflicts, trials, and testaments were identical to those in Midgard (where the human mortals dwelled). There were tales of Loki's jealousy, envy, and trickery. Thor bore unfathomable strength and power yet still to be burdened with the conflicts of his brother. All the while he was battling his pride and arrogance and lessons of humility. Yet he still was expected to remain steadfast to aid in his father Odin's vision.

Thor, Odin, and Loki were immune to the mortality of life in Midgard, but they were not immune to the trials and tribulations of all humans. It's as if the oral and written traditions of the Asgardians were to convey a deeper human purpose that could only be absorbed in allegory.

The unfortunate demise of the realm of Asgard, known as Ragnarök, was predetermined. Yet despite the wisdom of those residing in Asgard and the Norn's council, Odin felt compelled to prevent it. Ironically, the actions that he would conduct in retaliation would ultimately result in the fulfillment of the prophecy itself.[14]

The concept of personal destinies, the realm of Asgard (a Heaven that still managed to involve conflict), and gods who faced the same burdens as man was a romantic ideologue for me.

On March 13, 2020, the world as we knew it came to a standstill. Humanity was faced with a common foe for the first time since the devil himself. As though it were a war, we all endured survival through personal battles. I am referring to The Covid-19 Pandemic, of course.

Headlines were taken in siege and hostage by the "latest and greatest" breaking theology of the novel virus. We didn't know to wear goggles, gloves, or hazmat suits at first. Like many, I faced an acknowledgment that I had mistreated my personal well-being prior to the days that the virus emerged. I was indulgent. I ate foods that were sugary and fatty. I was not in touch with what my cholesterol levels even were.

My family and I fell ill. But the headlines were mostly filled with fear and uncertainty. Testing was not even available at that time. But it was a general conception that traceability had been conducted, and the threat of infection was eminent, but not yet out of control. Or so we would have liked to think, so we weren't sure if we had the novel *COVID-19* or some kind of flu.

I would attribute the illness that we all had as being one of the worst I had endured. The virus favored individuals who weren't at their peak well-being. After a week of fevers and severe congestion, we finally were able to move about. Yet seriously fatigued, very compromised, and had lingering symptoms that lasted for months. I was almost certain that we had contracted the virus known as COVID-19. It was very similar to all the headlines. But there wasn't even testing. How are we to be sure? We couldn't be sure.

However, I knew for certain two things. It was the worst I have ever felt. So, it was either Covid or potentially rivaled to be just as bad, and I came to fear contracting either. I viewed becoming reinfected as an almost certain death. This fear wasn't uncommon or irrational. Most people felt they had a reason to fear it; some feared it for good reasons. I wasn't necessarily the unhealthiest, but I knew that I hadn't done my body the service of being well-positioned to fight it if I was to be infected.

I let this fear govern me. Again, I do not think it was a struggle that I faced alone. In some regards, I felt my fears may have been disproportionate to the probability that I would be another casualty. I would save face and act in denial when confronted by colleagues. We all had to act tough anyway. Unfortunately, political narratives clouded productive recourse during the pandemic, and disinformation was prevalent. It was tough to navigate at times.

I came to explore this fear through my comprehension of Norse Ancient Mythology. After all, it was a significantly different outlook from that of Christianity. It appeared the Norse did not fear death, but rather, they embraced it. Death was just a conclusion of destiny. This much at least seemed logical to me as it is the curse that all men must face. In the end, nobody escapes death. Not even the Egyptians—with their pursuit of Alchemy and monolithic structures—ever found the key to immortality[3a].

However, it was not "death" that I feared. As I figured, I would not be cognizant of it, and after some time, it most likely wouldn't hurt at all. Yet I have many obligations and two sons to continue my name. Have I had enough influence on them? Can I assume they will conduct a life of decency? Was I effective in inspiring them? Most importantly of all, would they suffer more than the grief of my loss? Would they have adequate resources henceforth? Would they be predisposed to good opportunities for their futures?

Furthermore, I realized the things in my life that weighed heavily on my waking thoughts. Would my life have no real impact on my legacy following my death? Was I effective enough in my career that my peers and colleagues may look upon me with fondness or recall me with resentment? Were the investments and projects that I had started with the intention of accomplishing remarkable things or just left undone? Would all my dreams and ambitions be personified and gathered around me on my deathbed, forsaking me for never giving them an opportunity to live and thus die with me?

Moreover, I wonder if I would spend my eternity as a ghost, as an onlooker slightly out of reach of my loved ones. A ghost constantly tormented with ineffective ability to influence, despite my life's self-ordained duty to implement wisdom as their father. Or will I simply just perish? It occurs to me that I don't remember what came before this life, so why would I think that I would be aware of what came after? On most nights, I can't recount my dreams, so when I awake, it almost seems as if a piece of time was taken from me. Maybe this is all that we have? Perhaps there is nothing more.

Eventually, I came to realize that my pursuit of life was to self-prescribe an antidote of indulgence rather than face the truths that were much harder to swallow. This predisposed me to an existential crisis during a time when the world had stood still. Who are we to think that death would be a negative experience, as no one has ever tried it and reported otherwise? So, is there certainly anything to fear?

As I slowly unpacked all these questions that didn't have answers, I came to decide that it was not that "death" I feared most but that I have lived a life that I felt lacked appreciation of itself. As the Vikings would have asserted, if I carry out my destiny, there is no reason to think that death should be anything to fear. If the Norns have assigned you an ultimate calling, and you answer it, why would you not rest easy?

The Stoic philosophies of Seneca[6g] provide great serenity for some of these uncertainties in life. According to Seneca, Philosophy, and the studying of it, was a way to acquire the wisdom that one would receive in time anyway, but on an expedited timeline. Stoicism was an active participation in pursuing one's death by this philosophy.

The stoics were often accused of being apathetic, as they were viewed as having nonconstructive emotional responses as an unsuitable mechanism for dealing with life conflicts. When confronted with hardship, the Stoics would simply remind themselves that in the grand scope of time itself, our existence is akin to a mere moment or few seconds. This modest outlook should serve as guidance whenever the burden of suffering befell an individual.

I find these guidelines for life more compelling than Christian dogmas. The assertion that we must spend our entire lives in surrender and servitude to the One and Only—or face an eternity of suffering beyond this life—was never the stronger appeal. After all, is that not what we are doing here? Do we not suffer daily?

I often viewed the Bible as a device that was manipulated for political gain. What better way to guarantee the masses would be subordinate than to threaten them with the uncertainty that follows their death? After all, you can punish and persecute a man or force them into slavery. But once he is dead, you can no longer control him. But if he has not died before, then he has no reason to believe otherwise what lies beyond life.

We tend to allow the system to father us. As children, we may retaliate but become confronted in consequence by the logic of our parents. This conditioning leads many to believe that authority is an attribute of time. Therefore, when we become parents ourselves, we naturally assume the role of authority in turn. Often, there are innate playbooks in the hierarchal roles of our home, and life's discourse is predicated on the patterns we have observed in adolescence.

In other words, as a parent, if you were raised with the idea of absolutism, you may tend to implement rules that demonstrate your authority. Sometimes, these rules serve no purpose other than to remind your subordinates that you are in charge. This relationship serves no value beyond the order of the immediate future. No admiration or inspiration can be attained from such an environment. In fact, the only thing that it could tend to produce is a propensity to be a replicated pattern in the following generation. If anything, in the immediate future, only resentment will ensue.

An individual who has experienced oppressive subordination will often expect the same authority they once endured when their turn comes to lead. This creates an intriguing dynamic when the subordinate reaches the level of authority their parent once held—especially if that parent is still living.

Because modern life expectancy far exceeds that of past generations, we inherit social structures that are unfamiliar to those who came before us. In many ways, we are still piloting a social experiment—outliving the generations that shaped us and confronting new, untested hierarchies in the process.

Let us say that subordinate children become more sentient as adults. Though they may have exhibited mostly docile tendencies throughout childhood, suddenly, the child becomes empowered with authority. Such dynamics may challenge the paradigm that their still-living parents uphold. If a compromise cannot be made, their relationship will surely be compromised as a consequence. As if we assume that our children do not know what is best for them, and we as parents must exhibit our authoritarianism until our children are old enough to think for themselves. But how do we come to this conclusion, if we never allow the child to think for themselves?

As I said before, we let the system father us. The construction of heaven and hell merely serves as an existential threat to reinforce innate moral constructs that we are all born with anyway. We don't really need to tell our children that murder is bad; they seem to have a natural capacity for comprehending this.

So, if we know that murder is bad, why would we need to believe in heaven and hell? That's because the dilemma incites a need for practice and principle. As mentioned in the last chapter, the mind is a vacuum. Sometimes, we do not implicitly understand our interests, but it's almost as if they choose us. Without a religious construct, we have a void. So, the issue arises: what self-indulgence and lack of principle would drive a vehicle with no sense of navigation?

Sports entertainment is a massive industry. How would we come to create such elaborate infrastructures? The Romans would attribute the impact of gladiators and other events in the Colosseum[3c] as a means to satisfy and occupy the masses. How destructive would little boys be if they did not have an outlet for the primal aggression that they are predisposed to biologically? Additionally, it seems that religion is just another construct of controlling the masses, just as sports may be a way to curtail similar aggressions. The Christian Religion was the Order to the Chaos that would otherwise consume us.

Through my exploration of Norse mythology, I find myself yearning to comprehend how my innate moral foundation (being that of Christian ideology) would go on to believe such a "one and done" policy. Would it be non-compelling to admire fine art, understand sacred geometry, observe the great pyramids, or map the stars and accept that we weren't divine in some way? Were we just born to be subordinates of all that is glorious yet still be resolute of it all?

It seems that just as our desires beckon us, we know the difference in the boundaries of our consumption. Jordan Peterson would present the point: because a child likes cake, and it makes them happy, we know that giving a child nothing but cake, is not in their best interest.

I thought this was a perfect example of the value of abstaining from pure indulgence. However, what do we think about the knowledge that we consume? Surely, we can be captivated by nostalgia, brought to tears by a masterpiece, and have our hair stand on end as we listen to a beautiful music movement. However, just as we crave indulgence in the physical form, our metaphysical beings crave things too. Our muses pull us towards the things that animate our very souls.

Enigmas, incantations, symbols, and artwork help establish our point in the universe and our relationship with it. These things surely nourish us, too. In my pursuit to seek further enlightenment, I sought to join one of the world's oldest fraternities.

Not long after the birth of my second son, I was ceremoniously *"raised"* as a third-degree Master Mason. The world of Freemasonry[5c] was an enigma to me. From the outside, the Masons claim there is no Illuminati conspiracy; maybe the secrecy was the most alluring aspect. I was determined that the rite to enlightenment was my axe to grind, and somewhere hidden in the guise of that secret society were the keys to unlocking it all.

Freemasonry occasionally gets a bad rap. This is to be expected when you form a guild of secrecy. Outsiders may come to expect the worst. Yet despite these conspiracies, a robust and informative wealth of information is available online for anybody of curious mind and by little effort to obtain.

It is this new transparency that will yield the unfortunate demise of this ancient fraternity. For hundreds of years, the secret order of the Freemasons has captivated and attracted those willing to dance with its' secret oath. Yet, in the modern day, you can be curious and not follow through the laborious ceremonies to become indoctrinated into its society; it's no wonder the Freemasons dwindle in popularity.

To my dismay, there was not a lot of philosophy beyond the rituals. The initiation seems to uphold more enigma than the routine meetings, which typically consist of business-related housekeeping measures. Members would vote on simple and inevitable tasks of paying the electric bills, fixing a leaking faucet, and the costs associated with it.

Occasionally, an act of philanthropic service by means of fundraising for a community event was held. Not only were philosophies and greater truths not the subject of our meetings, but they were also inherently forbidden, as discussions of politics and religion were not permissible in the lodge. This rule was established to ensure brotherhood among those who may bear inconsistent ideologies with one another.

The only real parameter to your pledge was you had to proclaim an oath to a monotheistic entity. Examples given were those of typical Christian, Jewish, Muslim, and the like. Basically, if you were any sect of the Abrahamic Religions you were allowed in the club, providing you had strong references and passed a background check.

For the sake of participation, I proclaimed my oath, *"in the name of God."* I was never challenged on my claim, yet I would've had a difficult time explaining where I stood on the matter. At this time, I felt sort of "Agnostic." I felt that if there were a god, his comprehension would have exceeded the faculties of our minds. So, tongue-in-cheek, I didn't necessarily lie. As I said in the previous chapter, atheists were only in existence by opposition. If "heresy" was the only precursor that would indicate "Atheism," then it was validating the religion with its opposition.

So, at this point in my life, I was more than willing to hang my hat on a divine theory of agnostic belief. To me, there was a higher power, but it wasn't worth talking about because there's no way we could comprehend it. Therefore, there was nothing more to discuss. There could not and should not be a white-robed grandfather figure floating in the sky, though.

My masonic pursuits led me to stumble upon an intellectual figure by the name of Manly Hall[6h]. Manly was Masonic himself, and not afraid to explore the metaphysical world. Though he spoke on a variety of subjects, one particular of interest was Rosicrucianism[5d].

Like other sects of Christianity, the Rosicrucians had their own perceptions of the gospel. What started as a subculture of underground committees to discuss their intellectual adaptations of Christianity, the Rosicrucians came to terms that orthodox principles of heaven and hell were not absolutes. Rather, instead they came to uphold a model that was more similar to reincarnation as the Buddhists might allude to. Side note: Buddhists may attest that Buddhism is not necessarily a religion but a path to enlightenment[6i].

According to Manly, it was assumed that as we proceed birth, we spend nine months suspended in a state of purgatory, which cleanses us of the experiences of our preceding life, so we enter a new one as if we had amnesia. The cycle completes upon death as a spirit enters a nine-month limbo to process the course of their lives.

The value of reoccurring carnations would be to incite a Spiritual Transformation as if our souls had a predetermined caloric requirement and needed sustenance to meet their ultimate form. The pursuit of such wisdom and enlightenment could only be obtained through the suffering and virtues of those shared here in the flesh. Yet no one life had the required sustenance to fit the needs of a completed soul, and thus, there were multiple incarnations required to achieve the final result.

This model spoke to me as it seemed more like a process of self-improvement, as opposed to an unforgivable assessment of one's transgressions upon death. For the time, I considered compromising my Agnostic ways and subscribing to this ideology.

It seems a more righteous path than the Nordic philosophies of rape and pillage, steal, and covet, yet proclaim their actions were a valiant hero's effort. *"Just another day at the office!"* or *"All in a day's work!"* I imagine them hanging their hats at the end of the day. After all, what was most appealing to the Norse was their lack of fear surrounding the subject of death.

If I were to die tomorrow, would my children describe me as a Machiavellian[6j] type individual who feared not his mortality and who was more than willing to bend the rules to make everything better for us? Or should the structure in which I build my life be based on modesty, humility, meekness, and selflessness? Neither really seemed the standard I wanted. Why should I be a selfless punching bag for the powerful, and why should I exceed at the expense of another?

I do, however, feel I exhaust more effort to comprehend a matter than what should be a practical standard. For me, there is nothing harmonious about unanswered questions. Furthermore, the shattered remains of an orthodox theology—of a God I killed—still haunts me. I reassess: *Do I fear death? Do I fear living a life devoid of sustenance?* Or am I, *perhaps, simply too embarrassed to meet my maker?*

Brahman – *Coniunctio*

One of the oldest practiced religions is Hinduism[8b], and with more than 1 billion followers, it remains one of the dominant religions in the modern era. Western perceptions commonly misconceive Hinduism as a polytheistic religion. However, the truth is slightly more complicated yet more monotheistic than most may realize. To the Western mind, a common ignorant belief is that Eastern religions confide in contriving legions of enumerable and irrelevant gods.

Unlike the singular Bible in Christianity, there are more than six books and scriptures that serve the Hindu faith. Granted, the bible is technically a canon of books, but in contrast, the Hindu Mahabharata is the longest epic poem, with an estimated 1.8 million words comprising it. The Bible, still an impressive length, only possesses about 783,000 words, making the former about 2.3 times larger.

However, the Mahabharata is not the solely observed doctrine; there are others, and this is because, in Hinduism, there is more than one way to achieve Nirvana or Oneness. The Bible's New Testament presents only one solution to salvation, and that is "through the Son."

The most notable scripture is the Bhagavad Gita, likely due to its reference to Western atomic advancements. The "Gita," as often simplified, is the most influential section of the larger Mahabharata. The Gita is not absolute, it is a small section within Mahabharata.

Robert Oppenheimer[7e], the American theoretical physicist also declared the *"father of the atom bomb,"* made his infamous claim when observing the first atomic detonation: *"...Now I am become Death, the destroyer of worlds."* So, it seems that CERN was not the first to reference Hinduism in the field of nuclear research, as we established earlier.

However, the literal translation of *"Now I have become Death"* is up for dispute as some scholars would conclude that the translation goes, *"Now I have become time, the destroyer of worlds..."*

With either regard, we are confronted with an ominous tone of destruction regardless. However, there is much significance to the dialogue of the Bhagavad Gita at this point in the narration. Those famous lines attribute the entire piece to eminent entropy if they were someone's sole takeaway of the Gita. Before we unpack it, let's dissect the premise of the Gita.

As stated, the Mahabharata is the longest epic poem ever written. As the Hindu legend goes, it took 600 years to write the 100,000 verses of this epic between two ancient families at war, as depicted, taking place in approximately 3000 BC. The Mahabharata exists today, and its written existence is over 2500 years old, but it existed in oral traditions long before.

In contrast, the poem outdates the modern bible, but the stories are of antiquity, so much older that they exceed their current form. Its origins took place further from written conception than the work itself has aged today. Since it contains over 1.8 million words, it would take the average reader over 50 straight hours to read in one sitting.

The Bhagavad Gita is a small work with a personal dialogue. At the beginning of the Epic, two families, the Pandavas and the Kauravas, dueled in what was recorded as the Kurukshetra Wars[3d]. In the Gita, the epic's protagonist, Arjuna, was the third among the five Pandava brothers. In the opening, Arjuna declares he is *"tired"* and lays down his bow. His intentions were peace and to no longer feud with his cousins. The charioteer of his coach then begins a dialogue with him. The driver of this chariot identifies himself as Shri Krishna, and the two share a profound dialogue, which would be recorded as the *Bhagavad Gita*. The term *"Bhagavad Gita"* translates to *"The Divine Song."*

Shri Krishna (or Krishna) is often portrayed as a young man adorned with fine attire, flowers, and a very apparent trademark of having "blue skin." Blue skin is an exceedingly rare but naturally occurring condition known as Methemoglobinemia, in which the patient has a blood disorder resulting in an abnormal production of methemoglobin. The result causes blue pigmentation of the skin.

The most infamous of this condition occurred in a small population in Kentucky when a migrant couple settled, and both possessing the gene had given birth to seven children, of which four had blue skin. Ancient Hindus probably held such anomalies with a higher stigma than others of traditional pigmentation. Even in the modern age, anomalous births of conjoined twins may be heralded as an incarnation of the deity Shiva in some Hindu communities.

The Gita was not a standalone doctrine; however, many of its points may be assumed as so. The documentation of the Kurukshetra Wars will uphold it as a factual event; the narrative of the Gita can be layered as both an allegorical and literal piece. The dialogue becomes more abstract as Krisha soon reveals to Arjuna that he, himself, is the incarnation of the great supreme being. Deities and demigods were not an uncommon thing for the Hindus. However, Krishna makes it clear to Arjuna that all other demigods before him are manifestations of him.

This can be confusing on the surface, but simply put, the Hindus believe in a great supreme being, a Godhead. This Great Godhead is the omnipotent entity responsible for everything. It comprises not only God but the nature of all life forms. The Hindu Godhead is referred to as Brahman and takes several forms. Brahma, Vishnu, and Shiva comprise the

Brahman. However, in the Gita dialogue, the supreme being presents himself as Krishna. The beginning of this chapter referred to this chapter stated Hinduism was a monotheist religion and this premise is why.

The deity gods such as Shiva, Vishnu, and Brahma are often lumped into polytheist conceptions, but these deities merely comprise the Godhead, and none are absolute. They are adaptations and representations of the singular and infinite godhead, Brahman. But for all intents and purposes Krishna is Brahman but will be referred to as *"Shri Krishna"* or simply *"Krishna"* throughout the Bhagavad Gita.

So as Krishna continues to explain to Arjuna, many secrets of the cosmos are revealed to him on how to live a pious life. As stated before, there are several "paths" in Hinduism that one can take. These Paths are often referred to as different *"Yogas"* or practices. In modern Western culture, *"yoga"* is a strength training exercise used to tone and condition the body. In Hinduism, the physical prowess of *Yoga* is a mere fraction of the practice or practices therein.

There are four main paths of Yoga: *Karma Yoga, Bhakti Yoga, Raja Yoga and Jnana Yoga.* Each path is a different road to the same conclusion, that desired conclusion being *Nirvana* (aka heaven).

Karma Yoga is the most recognizable, and the premise is that the road to enlightenment may be achieved through good actions. This is the most common perception of yoga as we come to know the moral maxim of *"do unto others as you would have them do unto you."* It is the basic assertion that the world is what you put into it.

The path of Jnana is achieved through the intellect, and one is to attain wisdom to find Nirvana. This practice accepts the Brahman construct and recognizes the Atman (the self) and that the world is Maya (an illusion). The path to Nirvana through Jnana is through discipline and a life of humility.

Raja is achieved through meditation, as it recognizes the mind as the best tool for Enlightenment. Raja is the practice that presents the cultural adaptation of Yogic strength training, as holding poses for extended periods requires a strong core and peak physique. Those practicing Raja are akin to monks.

For the most part, Krishna's message is a proponent of Bhakti yoga, which is the Yoga of devotion. As Krishna would elude in his dialogue with Arjuna, he is the personification of the supreme one. He offers a path to Enlightenment by devotion to him alone, for it is the will of the divine that we all must execute.

Arjuna's position is that of Karma Yoga at the beginning, and he sees no greater good in destroying his cousins in battle. However, it is revealed to him, as Krishna takes his greater form and elaborates that he was time itself, the destroyer of worlds, and will annihilate with or without Arjuna as it is his will.

The core message of the Gita was not one of annihilation. However, Krishna does reveal that one shall not kill, but if one bears witness to a crime, it is their duty to be vigilant. Moreover, it was our responsibility to carry out our duties, not by attachment to the results, but because it was the will of Krishna.

Christianity wasn't the only faith to adopt a Christ figure as the term *"Christ"* itself was derived from the Greek word *"Christos."* Therefore, it can be inferred that the modern observance of *"Christ"* or *"Christos"* in Greek was taken from the playbook of the even older ancient scripture.

Etymologists will discount the terms *"Christ"* and *"Krishna" as directly tangible, as they arose from separate Proto-Indo-European roots despite having similar-sounding* phonetics. However, the concepts of both figures would associate them more closely. Both Christ and Krishna prophesize that the road to eternal prosperity may be obtained exclusively through acts of devotion. In turn, those practicing the faith may be able to receive serenity for the burden of conducting their daily functions. Both religions provide value to the nuances of moral virtue that cannot be remedied with prior blanket theisms.

However, not all sects of Hinduism follow the course of Bhakti Yoga and instead seek enlightenment by the path of renunciation, i.e., monks. This is to abstain from all activities to pursue the light inwardly. The goal of this is not by means of indifference but through the loss of self. An absolution of oneself results in one's integration with the great Brahman or the void of the unknown.

Even the path of devotion to Krishna will assume that we shall be consumed in this same void. This Bhakti practice promises that through a path of devotion, we may arrive at an "Ego Death" akin to the Jnana path.

As Alan Watts[6a] would attribute, the Western man says, "I am God," and he is locked up. Yet to the Hindus, if you said, "I am God," they would just ask you why it took you so long to figure it out. According to Watts, the struggle of modern man is that he assumes he is not made of the same stuff as the rest of the world. It's as if objects, people, and the world itself were something not of us but, in essence, to the Hindu: we are all one being. Now postulate: why would we have any individuation whatsoever?

His example was as follows: let us say that you could go to sleep and control your dreams. In each dream, you could dream of an entire lifetime. One night of sleep was a lifetime of 70 years. You can have everything you want and control everything. You control everything in this dream as though you are Brahman itself; you can be anything you want.

Now, say you did this for a long time. Each night is a different dream. Eventually you would choose to let this unfold with chance. You would release that control and see where the dream takes you. A divine entropy. Thus, we have our individual stories, and they all play out as if we are a theatre for the divine.

The Deities of Brahman are manifestations of the supreme being, as are we, each unique, no two stories the same, all personifications of the void and destined to return to it once we complete our divine dance. In the grand scheme of religions of antiquity, we have a value of blanket moral maxims. However, slightly newer (2000-2500 year old) philosophies are emerging that offer serenity for the nuances of life's tougher questions.

How do we find serenity for that which is a necessary function of human experience? Are sin and pragmatism not essential to living, lest we all become monks to resist that which cannot be abstained from?

Gnosis – *Fermentatio*

The story of Jesus and the Christian God is ubiquitous. Christianity is common among Westerners and almost every other culture worldwide. As of the 21st century, it is seemingly losing relevance in modern Western cultures.

What is not ubiquitous in the modern era is the Apocrypha[5e], the excluded texts of the Bible. The King James Bible is comprised of 66 books. In contrast, one canon of Apocrypha currently in Covent Presses' 2022 publication of The Complete 54-Book Apocrypha contains 54 books, as noted in the title. There are larger published archives of Apocrypha; however, substance tends to come at the cost of sustenance when it comes to these types of doctrines. Not to say that this collection could not or would not expand, but it is not a daily occurrence we find *Dead Sea scrolls* or other Gnostic Scriptures.

I want to talk about the Gnostic scriptures found in Nag Hamadi in 1945. The scrolls unearthed that day would shatter the paradigm of Christian philosophy if included in the original Bible. In fact, the pursuit of suppressing such doctrines and ideologies was highly controversial and quite the power struggle when we look at the history and the bloodshed that occurred when Roman influence prevailed at the end of the Ptolemaic Dynasty[3e].

Reading these scriptures in the modern day without persecution would be unfathomable to those seeking to protect it during those times. The sad irony that the scrolls would be unearthed in an ancient junk yard of ruins in Egypt is a somewhat noteworthy fate for these doctrines.

According to the Gnostics, God was not reduced to such a simplistic monotheistic form as he is today, and the scriptures found in Nag Hammadi present a slightly different adaptation of the Book of Genesis. Similar to the modern and commonly accepted version of Genesis portraying Adam and Eve, the story unfolds with a new perspective.

The Gnostic Genesis starts with the one true God, great in all its glory and infinite. However, the concept of this one true god is not quite the same context as the Christian God almighty commonly acknowledged. "*God*," also to be associated with the term "*Godhead*," a complex being, that of infinity and comprised of everything. No personifications can ever describe the Godhead, yet for context, "*God*" was defined as being comprised of 12 Æons. Each Æon can be attributed to a compartment of the cosmos, each unique and representing an attribute of the great Godhead. Our star Æon of this particular story, though, is named "*Sophia.*" Sophia translates from Greek to "Wisdom."

In a deep slumber, Sophia slept and, in her dream, had a thought, a "variant," so to speak, more closely resembling a nightmare. This nightmare was a manifestation of a Demiurge called *Yaldabaoth*. Now, Yaldabaoth was not a God in the Godhead sense, but his dedication was that of determination to have it be known that he was the Absolute God.

The Genesis[8a] story unfolds, but it is not the Godhead that created the known universe but Yaldabaoth who did; with his ignorance and desire to be all-powerful, he attempted to build a universe of his own to uphold this paradigm. His pursuit of creation faltered when he sculpted humans from clay, but they would topple over. No matter how hard he tried to contrive humans, his experiment would fail, and something was lacking.

Observing this, Sophia had sought to deceive her runaway variant, Yaldabaoth, by advising that he would blow some of his *"life force"* into his creation and it would be able to stand. Thus, it worked, and human life was born! Sophia's motives, however, unbeknownst to Yaldabaoth, were to instill the divinity of the Godhead in humans, for she knew that the goodness of herself and the other Æons was still within him and would transcend him into his creation despite his despicable nature.

Adam and Eve were created in his image, and they were directed to live a life in the Garden of Eden with the one rule: that they do not consume fruit from the Tree of Knowledge[8e]. However, Sophia felt primarily responsible for Yaldabaoth's existence and, therefore, obliged to incarnate herself as a snake that lured Eve to eat the fruit of the tree. The orthodox adaptation would make the snake an apparition of the devil, yet the role is uniquely played by the "good guy" in this instance. Classically, the serpent was a force of evil.

Eve was shamed, and she reasoned with Adam to indulge as well so they may suffer the same fate. Yaldabaoth was enraged upon discovering they ate the fruit; he rapes Eve and casts them both from the Garden of Eden.

As another consequence of Eve's defilement, she bears a child later born and to be known as Cain. Adam and Eve have a child of their own and name him Abel.

The difference between the two brothers' being Cain was comprised of rage, anger, and all the things Yaldabaoth was. Abel, being born of Adam and Eve, bears closer resemblance to the ultimate divinity. The two would later go on to quarrel, resulting in Cain's fratricide of his brother Abel. Though Abel was deceased, the bloodline of Adam was able to carry on through Abel's descendants. The Gnostics referred to these bloodlines as the Cainites and the Adamites henceforth.

The Gnostics believed that bearing the bloodline of the Adamites was a guarantee that your death would result in a return to the Godhead, which was the ultimate will of Sophia. It was a guaranteed absolution of life's sins and the right to eternal life beyond this world. The Cainites, however, would be predisposed to a life under the reign of Yaldabaoth's delusion. Reincarnation would be the result for Cains' descendants until every living being came to know the "Gnosis" and the one true God. This Gnosis was obtained by the Adamite bloodline intersecting the Cainite bloodlines in future generations and thus purifying it.

Several factions of Gnostics followed this original precursor of Genesis, yet the adoption of orthodox Christianity was not kind to any reasoning generally associated with a Godhead or something so closely representing Eastern cultures. I found this fascinating to think that early Christian Gnostics had a doctrine so strongly associated with Hindu "Brahman," as portrayed in the previous chapter. I was really scratching the surface upon discovering this, but I was not sure where it was heading.

There is no mention of Yaldabaoth, the Godhead, or Sophia in the widely accepted modern Bible. But for me, a key theme emerges. Yaldabaoth is more strongly associated with the God of the Old Testament as his typical rage and cognitive dissonance would allude. "Old Testament God" smites mankind by speaking multiple tongues as they attempt to build a tower to overthrow *Him*[8a]. He floods the earth when his creation gets away from *Him*, and let us not forget his forced covet of Eve at the beginning of the Gnostic story.

This type of crude Demiurge, "God-boy" behavior continues until the coming of Christ, in which even orthodox Christians would agree the narrative of God changes. No longer flooding the earth and striking lightning at anyone that takes his name in vain "New Testament, God" became benevolent and forgiving after the life and death of Jesus, his only son. No longer does the one-strike rule apply; sinners could be renounced of a lifetime of transgressions by taking the Lord to be their savior up until their final moments.

The Gnostic scriptures would portray the coming of Jesus himself as an incarnation of the Æon Sophia herself as a final effort to right her mistake known as Yaldabaoth. Prior to Christ, Heaven was a place far away, and only a life of perfection and total misery guaranteed you a ticket. However, it was the primary teaching of Jesus (Sophia) was that heaven was within us as the life of the Great Godhead had been blown into us upon creation, and thus, the keys to the kingdom of heaven were within us all along. This type of ideology was disruptive to the otherwise authoritarian Roman rulers. Their intentions persisted in the continuation of slavery, and thus, Jesus, aka Sophia, was crucified to be made an example of.

Some of the Gnostic scriptures get more and more abstract from there, but the Genesis I felt was significantly allegorical. It shifted the orthodox designations of Good and Evil in the Abrahamic religions. Gnostic scriptures were more parallel to Eastern religion than orthodox theologies. The orthodox model alluded to the fact that Eastern and Western models were only far contrasted with one another. Additionally, what was it about the birth and death of Jesus that caused us to view God as a kinder entity than his former self?

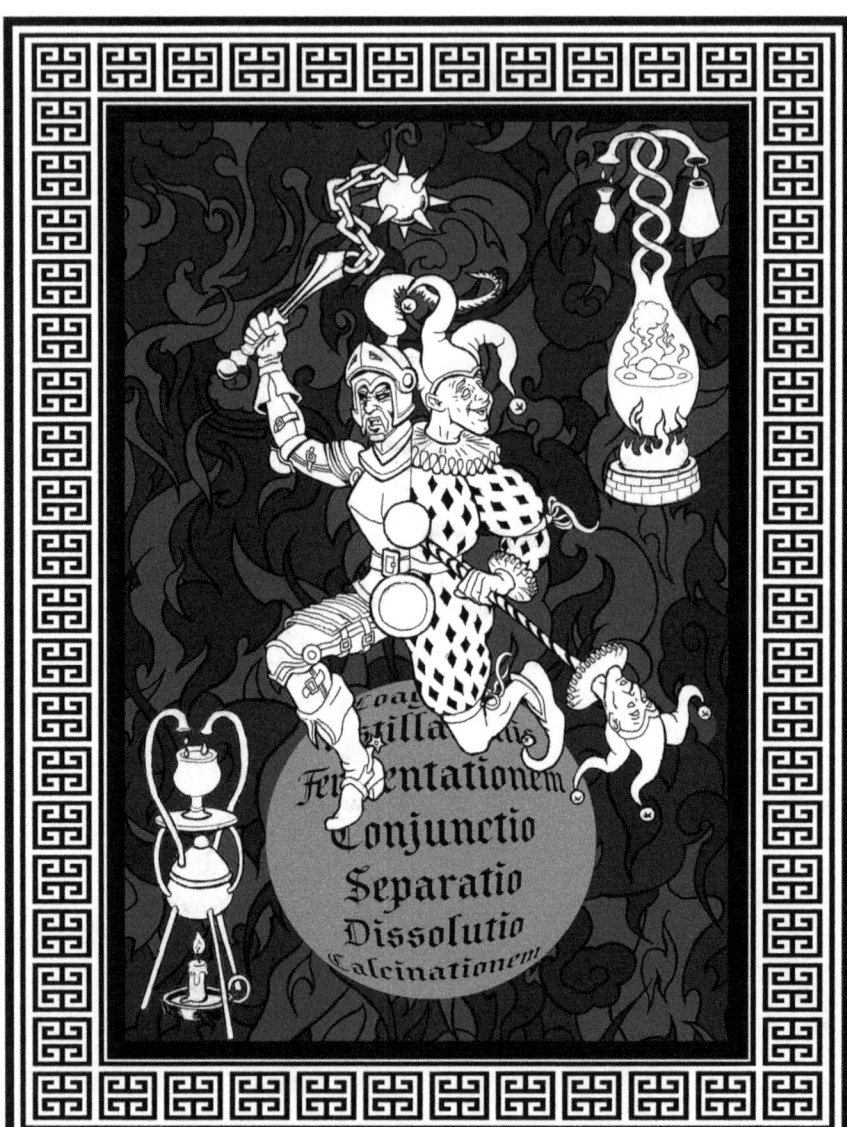

Jungian Principles – *Distillatio*

After learning about the Gnostic scriptures, I felt compelled to figure out what ripples it may have had on the world and potentially what the theory of Cainites and Adamites play on one's desire to take it literally and enact eugenics in its name. Was it to the detriment of society that Gnostic ideologies remain unorthodox or was it best they remain arcane to prevent scapegoating? Just how occult this was, and what influences would be the result of these ideologies?

The scriptures of Nag Hamadi were said to have been unearthed in 1945. However, its reemergence into the world was not a kind one. It is said that a peasant obtained the scrolls, they were mistreated and floated around the world for many years until a reputable museum was able to afford its price and preserve them. Like Hitler[3f] and his indoctrination by the *Protocols of the Elders of Zion*[5f], it may be best that the books found in Nag Hamadi remain arcane.

Historically, political factions have fabricated elaborate conspiracies with controlled narratives to create a scapegoat. This created the rise of fascism in Germany prior to World War 2[3g]. It has proven that when left unchecked, economic inadequacies can cause unwanted attention on an unsuspecting subculture or target. Perhaps compromising the vulnerable Cainite descendants was enough justification to keep it occult. This is, of course, my synthesis of the situation.

The Nuremberg trials followed the Holocaust, in which heinous acts of the Nazis were prosecuted for war crimes. Yet, to no real surprise, everyone on trial reportedly was just "following orders" from someone up the chain. So I asserted that if Hitler himself had he lived to see the trials, he would attest that it was his God-given duty to carry out the execution of 11 million unfortunate souls. However, he was not around to ask, as he had died. My research had concluded that the purpose of this evil was more laymen than I originally suspected.

"The battle line between good and evil runs through the heart of every man."

-Russian writer and historian Aleksandr Solzhenitsyn[4f]. Why would anyone purport that there was a shimmer of good in the heart of Hitler?

Just as we covered themes of Chaos and Order earlier in the book, man's capacity for evil often goes misunderstood, yet it is fascinating to us through our adaptations of graphic novels, horror stories, scary stories, and criminal documentaries. Our capacity for evil is often unexplored, yet the void of chaos is just as much a part of you as it is a part of Patrick Bateman in American Psycho. We can often keep those dark parts of ourselves at bay with vicarious adaptations of fiction without being Fascist dictators responsible for the murder of millions.

Before delving into the psychology of Hitler, let us cover some basic Jungian Principles to better get a scope of what would motivate Hitler to do such a thing. Carl Jung was a Swedish Psychologist who was a much younger friend and understudy to Sigmund Freud. The younger Carl thought of himself as an equal peer to Freud, yet Freud, however, regarded their relationship as more of a mentorship and saw himself as a paternal figure for the much younger Carl. This dynamic would seem to put a strain on their relationship later in life.

The key differences between Freudian and Jungian Psychologies[7a] are noted as Freud was more empirical and factual. Jung's philosophies were more abstract and tended to rely on mythologies, esoteric principles and be more radical than Freud's. Though more mystical in comparison, modern scholars and psychologists adopt a vast majority of Jung's work.

Most important were his attributes of what he defined as the "Self." Much like the previously noted Godhead, the "self" is comprised of several compartments of definition. Most notably the "Ego" and the "Shadow." Another adaptation of this polarity is indicated in the *Chaos and Order* chapter of this book.

According to Jung, the Ego is a self-aware compartment of oneself. It represents everything we outwardly portray ourselves to be or even as far as to say everything we consciously define ourselves to be. The "Shadow," on the other hand, lives just beyond our vision. Out of sight but not completely out of influence. The Shadow can implore our dreams with illusions or symbols. Also defined as that nagging and intrusive voice we hear sometimes but not exempt from serving as a moral conscience in the same capacity.

The Shadow is everything we can not fit into our "ego" due to social norms, dogmas, principles, or fear of losing oneself. Much like the Taoist pursuit to live in harmony with Wu-wei[6c], the merging of the Shadow and Ego is the optimal path to enlightenment for Jung's hypothetical modern man.

The theory is more empirical than we may acknowledge, and it is demonstrated in Jung's observation of primitive Aboriginals[7a]. Many of the primitive men he observed indicated an *"inner voice"* that, in contrast with contemporary man, would be the determination of utter insanity. These findings concluded that modern man had too many taboos to function the same as primitive man and was at a disadvantage by not listening to this inner voice, as he later defined as "The Shadow," due to these societal confines.

I should assert that *The Shadow* does not necessarily produce dark and evil influences exclusively in Jung's philosophy, but rather, it is a culmination of everything we are not. The Shadow's nature is depressed by societal influences. While

Western- contemporary individuals tend to associate these "darker sides" of themselves with the shadow, it is not intrinsically evil or bad by nature.

As we build upon the structure of Jung's "Self," we realize the Ego outwardly represents a "Persona." The Persona is not synonymous with the Ego, but it is defined by one's actions. The Ego, though influential in the Persona's capacity, is still heavily influenced by unconscious compartments of the self.

The Shadow, in a broader context, is also encompassed by the Anima or Animus. The determination of which is associated with the sex of the individual in observation. The male has an opposing force of the Anima, and the Female inherently has an Animus. So, along with the properties of the Shadow, a Male harnesses a repression of female energy and an unconscious state of affairs that goes along with it. A female possesses an innate suppression of Animus in addition. The opposite gendered parent directly influences these inherited properties. The pursuit of this spiritual Androgyny can be associated with the Rebis in Alchemy[5b], as discussed previously.

According to Jung, the Shadow would enact most of its influence while the individual slept. Subconscious desires and messages would reveal themselves to the sleeper through symbolism and cryptic messages of dreams.

The Shadow may directly or indirectly be responsible for the messages in dreams by a unifying aspect of the Self known as the *"Collective Unconscious." The Collective Unconscious* is a shared experience that all humans connect and are a part of. Of it: a stream of symbols, universal patterns, and values that illustrate our dreams and our purpose. The Collective Unconscious is a shared experience that we all experience individually.

Another way to look at the Collective Unconscious is to consider a baby when first born. Does the baby, lacking experience and life events, more or less a blank slate that's void of personality? Not really; according to Jung, some eternal patterns and Archetypes replicate themselves throughout the existence of time as if we come into the world with a bag full of personality functions that we unpack and bring into play as needed. Despite the multitude of these functions, we seem to always have a primary function.

The Myers-Briggs Personality Assessment[7g] is a commonly accepted adaptation of the philosophy of Archetypes. The scale of rating oneself is based on sixteen potential personality combinations dictated by the polarity of 4 main characteristics. The primary driver of each of the four characteristics is then expressed as four letters.

The First is whether someone is primarily introverted or extroverted, as exhibited by an "I" or "E."

The Second is whether one is intuitive or sensing, in essence, how they process the world. This is indicated by "N" or "S"— the N likely to not cause redundancy and confusion with the "I" signifying "Introverts in the first characteristic.

Third, we have a characteristic rating of "F" or "T" for the polarity between *feeling* or *thinking*; these are how one processes logical and emotional subjects.

Lastly, we have *Perceiving* vs *Judging* types where the subject holds disparity of their individual experience based on whether they inflict their rationale on the outside world or simply observe it. Any Combination of this test can infer a person's primary personality function traits yet inferior functions do apply.

For example, I am an ENTJ, and my inferior function is Introverted Feeling. In other words, if I had a bag full of Personality functions and I could try any one of them on: my ability to inwardly process my own emotions is my least stable function and tends to bring about my worst version of self. However, since I am slightly more extroverted and logical if I can rationalize it and share it, I tend to be living my best version of myself.

An interesting visual considers your primary function as the driver of an automobile; the person driving should always be your best. In periods of your best mental and physical health, you should assume it is. However, complex variables can push another function into the driver's seat. These may be fight or flight responses or reactions to external stimuli. My functionality with my inferior function driving is like letting a 4-year-old take the wheel; not a good idea, but if the optimal function is not available, these functions will step up.

Though Jung did not create the Myers-Briggs test, the spectrum of his Archetypes is based on it. Each Function is based on an Archetypal character that our collective unconscious shares. We all uphold these principles unknowingly, and furthermore, we represent these patterns in the stories we tell. The patterns of our stories tend to replicate themselves, too, as if there was an archetypal story wanting to tell itself over and over again.

Notable Archetypal characters include: "The Hero," "The Rebel," "The Ruler," "The Everyman," and "The Sage," just to name a few. Each one of these Archetypes can be associated with a Myers-Briggs type, and thus, you have a primary Archetype. Your aligned archetype is based on your rating of dominant characteristics within the 4-letter rating system.

Even the personification of Chaos and Order, as mentioned earlier, is an archetypal representation of Maternal and Paternal forces. The obelisks and pyramids are some of the oldest symbols we have of the two prominent Archetypes. One being phallic and the other uterine in nature[3a].

The chapter on Brahman illustrates the significance of our manifestations as incarnations of the Great Godhead. Yaldabaoth is an adaptation of Sophia's Wisdom.

Our abstracts of Religion are superimposed constructs of ourselves. None other than Odin would be a suited ruler for the Norse Mythology and Vikings of Midgard as his life was fated. He was an all too perfect Martyr for a Viking's life of violence and acceptance of their actions.

Even Satan himself was a "rebel" as he fell from Heaven in Milton's Paradise Lost[2]. In Satan's narrative, he was the oppressed and, by insurrection, sought to overthrow unjust authority.

An example of an Archetypal story of the *Hero's call to Action*[4c] plays as follows *(insert protagonist/ character flawed individual)* who sets out on *(insert journey, voyage or exploration)* to accomplish *(random goal or quest),* initially said individual is not prepared, yet encounters *(insert random Sage-like Archetype individual)* who elicits profound transformation of oneself and *(original character/protagonist)* identifies that they had *(insert initially unidentified attribute)* all along.

So, it is, therefore, not a change outside the protagonist but an inward Alchemical experience that transforms the protagonist into becoming the person they were meant to be at the beginning of the story. The protagonist then faces *(insert dragon, fear, or metaphorical monster)* to acquire *(insert: damsel in distress, gold, glory, or liberation.)*

I imagine that the last paragraph could postulate a variety of different genres and stories that you have read or seen. I could only hope that the completion of this book may illicit a transformation in the reader as you embark on this shared experience with me.

Now that we have covered Jungian psychology 101, what Archetypal character is Adolf Hitler? If Satan had an Archetype, you may postulate he was simply a rebel in Milton's story. However, you may be disgusted to determine Hitler was a "Hero" Archetype. I understand this is not a favorable Archetype for our villain here, so bear with me.

There is no real discernible difference between *Batman and the Joker*[1n]. They are the same, despite being an Antithesis of one another. They both have similar stories: the world abuses and hurts both of them. It is by catharsis that they either rise to the occasion to become their higher self by adopting their Shadow and become the character they were fated to become or deny integrating it. The only real underlying difference is that the good guy says: *"the world hurt me, I will stop it from hurting others,"* and the bad guy says: *"the world hurt me, I will hurt the world."*

Thus, we have Hitler's Archetype bound to him at birth, a destined hero who pursued Art school as his all too strict father ridiculed his every move. His Alchemical transformation was signified by his constant rejection to pursue his desired path, left homeless, and adopted by radical political movements that sculpted his sense of Nationalism to appease the never satisfied Paternal figure of his life.

It is apparent he likely carried heavy neurosis from these burdens. He went to War and fought with all his integrity to serve his country only to lose and return home soured, and with who to blame? The next discourse was to find a scapegoat for it all and so instilled his antisemitic ideologies.

Hitler's story was an unfortunate example of the extent one can go when consumed by their Shadow instead of integrating. The victims of the holocaust are the real heroes in retrospect; their story should never go untold, a senseless sacrifice to a villain's craze.

Hitler, though failing to adhere to a proper moral compass, was bound to his archetypal role. Was his role inherited because he answered the "call to action," and would the story have played out differently if he had faced the neuroses of his childhood traumas instead of becoming consumed by his shadow?

Catharsis – *Coagulatio*

The pursuit of Philosophy can be paradoxical. On one hand, you float off into the clouds with complex abstracts and get lost in alternate realities. On the other, you play a part; you play your role in the world, abiding by rules and social norms as if you were none the wiser. You function in your role as if no one knows the other role you play. Sometimes, strange coincidences emerge between these two worlds, acting as functional clues. They serve as answers to questions that are sometimes too complex to articulate.

I like to think these implications are signs from our Shadow or divine self that we are on the right path. It is this Synchronicity[7a] that drives philosophy forward. The universe is full of mysterious patterns, and their beauty is so profound if we can be articulate enough to capture them or lucky enough to bear witness without intervention.

I am grateful to have been drawn to a collective array of topics that instinctively help catalog the events of my own life. I feel the larger insights I was able to pull away from these studies helped unravel a deeper mystery of myself. The apotheosis of these experiences reminds me that the laws of the universe are undoubtedly just as equally superimposed. Perhaps metaphors and allegories are the only real way to digest the more complex and nuanced nature of our existence.

The experiences of mankind are shared, as I have come to learn, and the likelihood of our gods portraying our inner struggles was more prominent than I had previously realized. As I stated in the beginning, I would infer that all of this is connected. This was my existential crisis and moral dilemma embedded in my role as both a father and a son, in contrast. My journey was mostly self-guided and through chance and impulse to explore that which infatuated my mind, I believe I have derived a fated conclusion I would like to share.

Where I started: I struggled in my personal life with my relationship with my father and my journey to being the best father I can be for my children. It is as if we were expected to have the rule book ahead of time and know how to manage these raging seas.

But the lesson was clear to me now, and it took several years of following the impulses to find it. It is as plain as the nose on my face, much like Pinocchio[1m], the story of a wooden puppet who pursues an adventure in the world to demonstrate moral virtue and rescues his father from the belly of a whale in the end. I was the lost Geppetto in this story, consumed by the whale, yet as a father and a son I had to admit my role was just as much Pinocchio's.

Initially, I was just as lost as Geppetto at sea. I found myself superimposing paternal standards on other male figures in my life, just to be let down when they failed to reciprocate my requirements as if I were their surrogate son. I would try to seek solace and simulate my father upon them as if they had the answers I was seeking. Jung had struggled with asserting a Paternal order in his life with Freud. Perhaps his own—beyond basic—comprehension of the human mind may have potentially shortsighted the dynamics of his own life.

It was not the superimposed paternal figures that would save me in the end, but my release of the paternal logic I had of the world. It was this Patriarchal sense of order that conflicted with my ability to perform as a loving father. Additionally, resentment for the shortcomings of my father and my fall from faith were presumably all separate issues. Unbeknownst to me it was an archetypal message I had been oblivious to all along.

Therefore, in writing this, I relinquish the burden of an angry God's shortcomings, the eternal suffering and replication of my forefathers. I lay to rest the injustice for all the villains that bear their Hero roles with misdirection. Yet through all this, it is not the rite of paternal injustices but my finger that pointed at them. Today, I bury the dead God Yaldabaoth, who didn't have a fighting chance. Sophia deemed him an abomination from the start.

The Archetypal story of God's Catharsis was there all along in the Apocrypha text. Just as Pinocchio journeyed into the belly of the beast to save his father, so did the crucified Jesus, who lay ruined and nailed to a cross. Only by the loss of God's own son would he bear a misery only known to we mortals in prior contrast. A tragedy that was the catalyst of a necessary transformation.

Disintegration, absolution, and reincarnation, integration.

He, like all of us, is merely a dream of the Brahman, and the chapter of Christianity needs not to be an island in the sea of religions but a manifestation of the one true God. Nothing more, nothing less. It is all an ocean.

The fall of an era, the close of a chapter on all things Fatherdom, the sun now sets on the God of Abraham. These echoes of Archetypal tales were just one manifestation of it all: a zeitgeist[9j] bubbling below the surface waiting to be perceived. Begging for renunciation.

The catharsis Lester faced in American Beauty[1b] could not have been obtained without the intervention of Ricky, who served as a suitable son for Lester. The interactions of our children are what drive us to become a greater self. Parenthood positions us with the false narrative that we are the sole teachers of our kin, but the provocation of catharsis we receive in return is so much more if we would only listen. It's never too late for this transformation, as Fatherdom is bilateral.

Unlike the failed transformation of Patrick Bateman[1a], we persist where he fell short. And with this new Gnosis—"*[if] there is no catharsis, punishment will allude, and we gain no deeper knowledge of ourselves.*"

Bury your dead gods. Release your fathers of their sins. Break the chains that anchor your thrones. Your father's prison is waiting to be unlocked by his own son's key.

Saturnian Eulogy

Here it be, our father shall lie,
shallowed and hallowed,
at one fathom, plus five.

This place shall be his tomb,
not the ether of her oceanic womb.
For the waves would crush his bones to sand—
so let stone keep him intact, adorned, and named.

What started at Adam:
was a hunger—
should this be what survives him?

Cyclical as a default,

a devourer of his own kin,
yet it wasn't his fault.
Before him— was his own father's sin.

O, sons of Saturn!—
has Eden's fruit not fed you enough?
Or rather— has it borne too much?

Lest we sons leave nothing to rot!
Harness the excess and by our coffers it ferments.
That which we do not need today,
would otherwise be lamented tomorrow.

Alas! We are drunken and a darker truth reveals:
the tree was withholding!
This must be why we starve—
never shall we leave any on the branch.

Summon Orestes!
It is he that should remove the tree,
and drive his wedge within the root—
never again, shall it tempt thee!

This section provides references, clarifications, and sources for *concepts*, *quotations*, and historical *references* throughout *Fatherdom*. The alphanumeric code designates where the topic appears within the chronological order of the **Thematic Themes**.

1. **Contemporary Society**
    a) *American Psycho* (film 2000) based on the novel by Bret Easton Ellis, published in 1991. Depicting a Manhattan investment banker, Patrick Bateman, supposably living a double life as a serial killer.
    b) *American Beauty* (film 1999), a dark comedy written by Alan Ball about American suburban culture.
    c) *Food Delivery Services* - 3rd party services that bridge restaurant services to user users by providing integrated delivery services. i.e. *UberEATS, DoorDash.*
    d) *Prolific Serial Killers* (20th Century) - *i.e., Ted Bundy, Jeffrey Dahmer, Zodiac Killer*
    e) *TikTok* (mobile application) was formerly *Musically* released Sept 2016 by developer *ByteDance,* hosting short videos. Gained proliferation during the COVID-19 Pandemic.
    f) *The "L"* - Nickname for Chicago's transit system. The name *"L"* serves as a nickname describing its *elevated* construction.
    g) *Video Conferencing software* - i.e., Microsoft *Teams or Zoom.* Designed to provide video calling capability despite geographic challenges, which became more prominent during the *pandemic.*
    h) *Full House* (TV Show 1987-1995) ABC Network, a Jeff Franklin created a family-friendly sitcom

about a widowed father (Danny Tanner) raising a large family in San Fransico.
- **i)** *Facebook* (Social Media Platform) - founded in 2004 by Mark Zuckerberg and four other Harvard students, initially for student social networking, later expanded to be open to all.
- **j)** *Apple* (Technology Company) - products include *iPhone* and *iPad*.
- **k)** *TV Guide* (Media Company) - offers Television program information to consumers in exclusively digital format since 2006 but was primarily provided in print edition prior to the change.
- **l)** *Tupperware* - Founded by Earl Tupper in 1942. A company that produces residential kitchen storage solutions.
- **m)** *Tony Robbins* - American Author, success coach and public speaker.
- **n)** *Batman* (DC Comics) - Created by Bob Kane & Bill Finger. Bruce Wayne, a masked vigilante who fights crime under the guise of *Batman*. The major villain he faced was *Joker*, though there were many others.
- **o)** *The Adventures of Pinocchio* (1883) - originally written by Carlo Collodi in 1883, many new adaptations exist. A moral children's story of a puppet brought to life

2. **Cultural & Political**
   - **a)** *Totalitarian* - of or relating to centralized control by an autocratic leader or hierarchy. i.e., dictatorial or authoritarian. As per Merriam-Webster.

b) Saul Alinsky - an activist, writer and political theorist. His political ideologies often criticized by conservatives for inspiring radical left agendas.
  c) *Andrew James Breitbart* - Controversial conservative journalist. Founder of HuffPost and Breitbart News.
  d) *Protocols of the Elders of Zion*
3. **Historical Events**
   a) *Egyptian belief in everlasting life,* the Egyptians placed great emphasis on these themes. However, the thought that obelisks were phallic symbols and pyramids were symbolic uteruses is a creative interpretation. The builders' intended significance of these structures is part of the lure for Egyptologists.
   b) *Plague Doctor* - 17th century Europe: physicians who treated victims of bubonic plague, noted for their characteristic bird-beak-shaped masks.
   c) *Colosseum* (Ancient Rome) - Giant elliptical amphitheater which hosted dramatized reenactments and battles for entertainment of up to 80,000 spectators at one time.
   d) *Kurukshetra Wars* - a dynastic war between cousin families Pandavas and Kauravas for the throne of Hastinapura as depicted in the Mahabharata Epic. Historical accuracy is debated amongst scholars.
   e) *Ptolemy I Soter* - Successor of Alexander the Great as a Macedonian General. Pharoah of Ptolemaic Egypt from approximately 305BC-282BC. His descendants continued what is referred to as the Ptolemaic Dynasty until 30BC,

when Roman Imperialism suppressed anything but orthodox Christian religion.
- **f)** *Adolf Hitler* - Dictator of Nazi Germany. Died of suicide in 1945 in his bunker. Early biographical reports indicate he was once an aspiring artist with an estranged father relationship. He served in WWI and took Germany's loss personally; he fell into an antisemitic ideology that was rising in Germany before fully engaging with the Nazi party.
- **g)** World Wars I & II - the former initially called the "Great War" was a global conflict. Under Hitler's influence, the latter was ignited as a second global conflict. His party additionally performed systematic genocide of approximately 6 million Jews. The Nuremberg Trials were a series of 13 trials conducted by Allied forces for the war crimes of the Nazis.

4. **Literature & Art**
   - **a)** *Animal Farm* (a Novel, 1945) written by George Orwell. It was a direct critique of the Soviet Union under Stalin's rule. Additionally, there was a rise in anti-fascism in Europe due to the political climate of the Nazi party. Orwell was an anti-Marxist who wrote the cautionary tale to warn of the dangers of collectivism and how quickly it can turn into authoritarian rule.
   - **b)** *Walking on Sunshine* (song, 1985) written and performed by Katrina and the Waves, a British Rock Band in their self-titled album. The song topped the charts in several global markets.
   - **c)** *Call to Action* - the pivotal step in an archetypal process that author Joseph Cambell called *The Hero's Journey*. Cambell spent his life studying

myths and deciphering their framework into archetypal definitions.
d) *Creation of Adam* - Architectural painting on the ceiling of the Sistine Chapel. Fundamentally capturing the paradoxical relationship between man and his creator in Christian iconography.

4.6692) *Hellas* - Where is she?

e) *Rich Dad, Poor Dad* - personal finance self-help book by Robert Kiyosaki illustrating postulating that calculated risk and short-term disciplines in gratification make long-term prosperity.
f) *Aleksandr Solzhenitsyn* - Russian dissident and author exposing horrors of internment camps, notably in the book *The Gulag Archipelago*.

5. **Occultism**
    a) *Emerald Tablets* - a cryptic text written under the pseudonym of Hermes Trismegistus, the archetypal unity of 3 distinctly separate cultures: The Egyptian, Greek, and Roman mythologies. Hermeticism emerged during the Hellenistic Era but was suppressed under Roman orthodoxy.
    b) *Alchemy* - an ancient form of rudimentary or protoscience and philosophy that focused on the refinement of oneself and materials alike. The over-arching theme shares some unity; however, there are some nuances that segregate the esoteric and exoteric applications therein.
    c) *Freemasonry* - An ancient fraternity founded by a guild of stonemasons, operates today under obscurity. Themes of stonemasonry serve as metaphorical symbolism for the fraternity's pursuit of personal development. The initiation process is a dramatization of the Freemason's origin story, by which the indoctrinated member

has revealed their secrets through the oath of secrecy.
   d) *Rosicrucianism* - an occult spiritual practice that arose in Europe in the 17th century that focuses on esoteric Christian ideologies.
   e) *Apocrypha* - Biblical books containing Christian theisms not contained in the orthodox canon. Suppression of the doctrines purportedly due to their relevance or usefulness to the church or they lack authenticity. However, these claims tend to raise conspiracy and criticisms.

6. **Philosophy & Esoterica**
   a) *Alan Watts - Out of Your Mind* is a collection of audio lectures where Watts discusses Western existentialism and shares Eastern philosophy anecdotes.
   b) *Friedrich Nietzsche* - German scholar, philosopher, and writer. Revered by philosophers as one of the most influential thinkers of the modern era.
   c) *Taoism or Daoism* - the philosophical and spiritual tradition of Chinese philosophy promoting harmony with the Tao, which observes the nature of the universe as dual-natured. The thematic philosophy is iconized by the yin-yang. In *Daoism,* a state of effortless action or balance and harmony is identified with the concept *of Wu-Wei*.
   d) *Jordan Peterson* - Canadian conservative author and commentator specializing in psychology and focuses on cultural and political narratives. *Fatherdom* pulls ideas from diptych books: *12 Rules for Life: An Anecdote for Chaos* and *Beyond Order: 12 More Rules for Life.*

e) *Socrates* - Greek Philosopher c 470 BC – 370 BC. Believed to have inspired the principles of Western philosophy.
f) *John Milton* - 17th-century poet and author of Paradise Lost, which explores the temptation of Adam and Eve following the fall of Satan.
g) *Seneca, Stoic Philosopher* - 4 BC and 65 AD statesman and dramatist. Acted as counsel to Roman Emperor Nero until accused of conspiracy was sentenced to forced suicide.
h) *Manly P. Hall* - (1901- 1990) Canadian-born American Philosopher devoted to mysticism and esoteric philosophy.
i) *Enlightenment (Buddhism)* - Eastern Spiritual Philosophy often conflated with being a religion but rather a foundation of religious ideology based on the life experiences of Siddhartha, later known as the *Buddha,* as he achieved *Enlightenment.*
j) *Machiavellian* - Description of one's negative personality trait depicted by characteristics of deceit, manipulation, and self-interest. It is considered one of Paulhus & William's *Dark Triad* traits. The term is based on the philosophies of Niccolo Machiavelli's 16th century *The Prince.*

7. **Psychology & Science**
   a) *Carl Jung* - Psychologist, understudy of Sigmund Freud. Jung applied human experience to Mythology through a shared experience he called the *Collective Unconscious.* This shared experience is defined by *Archetypes, Symbolism,* and Jung's model of the self, which consists of a *Shadow* compartment. This polarized aspect of

the self was observed in a clinical study of Aboriginals in his book *Man and his Symbols* (published 1964), which was narrowly completed before his death in 1961.
   b) *Carl Sagan* - (1934-1996) American Astronomer and planetary scientist. Sagan had a successful career in academia, though he was open to the chances of extraterrestrial intelligence, which caused some scrutiny by cohorts.
   c) *CERN* - European Organization for Nuclear Research. It hosts the world's largest and most powerful particle accelerator.
   d) *Albert Mehrabian* - American Psychologist and communication expert
   e) *Robert Oppenheimer* - An American theoretical physicist and director of *The Manhattan Project. His oversight saw the production of the first atomic weapons*
   f) *Sigmund Freud* - 1856- 1939 Austrian neurologist and founder of psychoanalysis. His treatments aimed to target the unconscious repressions of an individual, and his influence is still relevant in the modern day.
   g) *Myers-Briggs Type Indicator* - Inspired by Jung's *Psychological Types,* (1921) Katharine Cook Briggs - a Swiss psychiatrist, and her daughter Isabel Briggs Myers. A test conducts binary values based on 4 categories.

8. **Religion & Mythology**
   a) *Christianity* - practice exercising the teaching of the Bible. Comprised of two major Testaments. The Old Testament establishes the creation of the world (Genesis), humanity's fall (Adam and Eve), divine judgment (Flood, Tower of Babel),

and the covenant with God. The New Testament centers on Jesus Christ as the Son of God, whose death and resurrection offer redemption. *Revelation* concludes with the final judgment and restoration of divine order.

b) *Hinduism* - One of the oldest and most globally practiced religions in the modern day, Hinduism is rooted in the Vedas and epics like the *Mahabharata* and *Bhagavad Gita*. It emphasizes dharma (duty), karma (action), and moksha (liberation). Central figures include Shiva (Nataraja, the cosmic dancer) and Krishna, with yoga serving as a spiritual path toward enlightenment. Nirvana represents the release from the cycle of rebirth (samsara).

c) *Norse Mythology* - Rooted in the ancient beliefs of the Scandinavian peoples, Norse mythology centers on the Allfather, Odin, who governs from Asgard. Yggdrasil, the World Tree, connects the nine realms, including Midgard (Earth). Key figures include Thor, the god of thunder, and Loki, the trickster. Ragnarök foretells the cataclysmic end of the gods, marked by the rise of Fenrir and the destruction of Asgard.

d) *Egyptian Mythology* - Rooted in the beliefs of ancient Egypt, Egyptian mythology features a complex pantheon tied to life, death, and the afterlife. Anubis, the jackal-headed god, presided over mummification and guided souls through the underworld. Myths centered on the divine order (ma'at), the struggle between gods like Osiris and Set, and the cycles of death and rebirth represented by Ra's journey across the sky.

e) *Tree of Knowledge & the Snake* - In *Judeo-Christian* tradition, the *Tree of Life* and the snake appear in Genesis. The Tree of Life symbolizes eternal life and divine wisdom, while the *snake* represents temptation and the fall of man, leading to humanity being exiled from Eden.
9. **Terminology & Reference**
   a) *Muse* - A term derived from Greek and Roman mythology. In the modern context, it is the term given an anthropomorphic force or creative influence sensed by artists, authors, and those involved in the creative arts.
   b) *Christian Popularity Census* - Conducted by *PEW Research Center*, a nonpartisan opinion polling organization aimed to capture demographical data for social science research.
   c) *Science* - a study of the world, an operating model based on structure and behavior of empirical and observable testing and indisputable facts.
   d) *Neonym* - a new or novel word. One that has not been accepted into the ubiquity of mainstream language.
   e) *Etymology* - a study of the origin and evolution of words in modern linguistics. By referencing a word's origin, its elementary meaning can be traced, not just the word form.
   f) *Epicurean* - A philosophy founded by *Epicurus* that embraces moderate pleasure and simplicity as the highest good. Often cited in reference to refined tastes, especially gourmet food.
   g) *Communism* - An ideology of economic and sociopolitical function developed by Karl Marx

and Friedrich Engels meant to dismantle private ownership and overthrow capitalist profit-based models.

h) *Parendom* - the name of a Daycare in Rennes, France. Inherently, the term is formed from the French words *Paren* and *Domicile*. This word was avoided as the book's title out of fear it may be conflated with the existing establishment.

i) *RAM (Random Access Memory)* - in computer systems technology, RAM serves as a temporary working memory for system processes.

j) *Zeitgeist* - a term that serves to dictate reflections of a cultural attitude, moral, or sentiment for a given *era* or timeline. Often called sited as the *spirit of the age*.

Where is Hellas?

www.ingramcontent.com/pod-product-compliance
Lightning Source LLC
Chambersburg PA
CBHW070636030426
42337CB00020B/4040